Supernatural Prayer and Fasting

The Keys to Triumphant Living

Richard Booker

Destiny Image Publishers

P.O. Box 310

Shippensburg, PA 17257

"Speaking to the Purposes of God for this Generation"

ISBN 1-56043-117-2

Library of Congress Catalog Number 93-072129

For Worldwide Distribution

Printed in the U.S.A.

First Printing: 1993
Second Printing: 1994

Destiny Image books are available through these fine distributors outside the United States:

Christian Growth, Inc.
Jalan Kilang-Timor, Singapore 0315

Lifestream
Nottingham, England

Rhema Ministries Trading
Randburg, South Africa

Salvation Book Centre
Petaling, Jaya, Malaysia

Successful Christian Living
Capetown, Rep. of South Africa

Vision Resources
Ponsonby, Auckland, New Zealand

WA Buchanan Company
Geebung, Queensland, Australia

Word Alive
Niverville, Manitoba, Canada

Other books by Richard Booker available from Destiny Image Publishers:

Come and Dine
What Everyone Needs to Know About God
Blow the Trumpet in Zion
The Miracle of the Scarlet Thread
Seated in Heavenly Places
Jesus in the Feasts of Israel
Radical Christian Living
How to Prepare for the Coming Revival

Acknowledgments

My love and gratitude to my wife, Peggy, for sharing with me this adventurous life of supernatural prayer and fasting. She's not only the greatest wife in the world, she is also the best Christian I know.

Thanks also to Don Nori for writing the Foreword. Your kindness is much appreciated. I am also grateful to Carol Olejnik for doing a great job typing the manuscript and to Alice Depot for her proofreading assistance.

Contents

Foreword

There are some folks who yearn for the nearness of the Lord and for the confidence that He has their best interest at heart. They want to serve Him and see the world change as they minister His Word and His power. Yet the surest way to separate the sheep from the goats is to bring up two small, misunderstood words: prayer and fasting.

I believe that the Lord has desires too. He wants to bless us and bring us into the fullness of His Life and power. He wants to give us the desires of our hearts. After all, He is the One who gave us those desires to begin with. *But He wants to do more than that.* He wants to make us effectual ministers of the gospel whether we are pastors, Sunday School teachers, homemakers, or career people. God wants a people through whom He can and will do His mighty will on the earth.

Prayer and fasting are two of our most powerful tools in our search for His fullness. In bookstores crowded with countless books on prayer and fasting, this new book by Richard Booker cuts through the haze, the confusion, and the outright error surrounding this subject. It sheds the fresh light of God's revelation on prayer and fasting. The *real key* to triumphant Christian living is to live, pray, and fast God's way instead of our own!

The heart of effective prayer lies in finding God's perfect will, and then co-laboring *with* Him in prayer to bring His will to pass on the earth! Can you sense the difference? Do you feel the anointing of our Father's presence on this "new" way of prayer? Isn't it about time for us to pray until we clearly hear our Father's heart, and then pray and fast until His will is done on earth as it is in Heaven?

In a Church generation bent on arm-wrestling, commanding, and convincing God to move to their tune and beat, *Supernatural Prayer and Fasting* brings a fresh wind of God to the Church, a holy wind borne on righteous prayer and filled with world-changing power and God-ordained priorities. If God's people will only heed the call to pray and fast in God's way, the world and the Church will never be the same!

Don Nori

Introduction

I'll never forget the day when, for the last time, I walked out of my office at the oil company in Houston, Texas, where I had been employed as a computer training and management consultant. I said my final good-byes to my co-workers, hurried to the parking garage, and with a sense of apprehension and uncertainty, carefully made the one-hour drive home through Houston's infamous rush hour traffic.

That drive seemed like an eternity as a multitude of thoughts raced through my mind—I had lectured throughout the United States, Canada and Mexico training more than a thousand management and computer personnel. More than 20 of my articles had appeared in leading computer publications. I was listed in *Who's Who in Computers and Automation, Who's Who in Training and Development* and the *Dictionary of International Biography*, and was a frequent speaker for the American Management Association.

As I neared my house, I didn't know what destiny awaited me. My successful business career was over, and I would never again return to that office. I had no bonds to cash, no stocks to sell, no savings to draw from, and now without the company benefits, there would be no insurance, hospitalization or any other financial benefits we Americans are accustomed to having. Neither would there be a regular paycheck.

I had read in the Bible how God called people to special tasks and gave them the ability and resources they needed to successfully carry out their assignments—but that was in the Bible! Was it possible that God still called people to do specific things for Him today? Would He provide for the needs of a twentieth-century American as He did for people in ancient times? More specifically, was He calling me to a certain task and would He meet my needs? I found the answers to these and many more questions through a life of supernatural prayer and fasting.

Now I pray that God will help you discover the answers to these questions for your own life as you begin an incredible adventure with Him in that same wondrous world of supernatural prayer and fasting.

1

Prayer—Our Contact With God

What do you think of when you hear the word *prayer*? To some it means chanting a religious phrase, repeatedly, in a monotone. To others it means silent meditation. I've always wondered how many people actually prayed when, at a public gathering, a leader called for a moment of "silent prayer." To some, prayer is what you do when you're in trouble. That was the way I used to think about prayer, particularly when I was a kid about to get a spanking. Or when I needed God to help me write a book—like this one, for example.

Because prayer means so many different things to so many people, we must begin our quest for supernatural prayer and fasting by defining exactly what we mean when we use the word *pray*.

What Is Prayer?

I have found the following definition of prayer helpful in my own life:

Prayer is communicating with God and is His normally appointed means for working out His redemptive plan and purposes for mankind.

First of all, prayer is communicating. Communicating is not something we humans do very well. This is particularly true when the opposite members of the sexes try to communicate.

I've been married to a wonderful woman for more than 26 years. Her name is Peggy. We're still trying to understand one another. I hear her words, but don't always understand her meaning. Maybe that's because males are left-brain oriented and females are right-brain oriented.

The left side of the brain houses more of the logical, analytical, factual and aggressive centers of thought. The right brain is the center for feelings, emotions and relationships. Husbands and wives often have verbal spats because they're talking out of different sides of their brains, not their mouths. This spat sometimes becomes a shouting match. (Never at my house, of course.)

Since we humans have so much trouble communicating with one another, it is no wonder that communicating with God can sometimes be difficult. Is God left-brain oriented or right-brain oriented? Of course God is both.

A key word in our definition is the word *normally*. The Bible tells us that God is self-sufficient and in need of nothing or no one. This means He can do His thing without our help. So, why doesn't He do it? The reason is He has chosen to let us participate or partner with Him in bringing His will from Heaven to earth. He decided, out of His own sovereign good pleasure, to let us in on what He is doing.

God is actually looking for people who will co-labor with Him in working out His plan and purposes for mankind. He is looking for prayer partners who will discern His will and then pray it from Heaven to earth. Even if we go through life without this realization and understanding, that doesn't mean God's purposes will not be accomplished. God will find someone else who will partner with Him. We will miss the exciting adventure of being God's prayer partner, but He will continue His program.

I believe the most important word in our definition is the word *redemptive*. To redeem something means to buy it back. For example, if you lost your property because you couldn't pay your mortgage, you could redeem it if you had the required amount of money.

The Bible says that all of humanity needs to be redeemed from the curse and bondage of sin. This redemption is made possible for us through the atonement (reconciling work) of Jesus Christ on the cross.

The apostle Peter wrote, "Knowing that you were not redeemed with corruptible things, like silver or gold, from your aimless conduct received by tradition from your fathers, but with the precious blood of Christ, as of a lamb without blemish and without spot" (1 Pet. 1:18-19).

By His very act of creating us, God can claim ownership of us. Satan, however, deceived our first parents. When Adam and Eve sinned, we became lost from God and in need of salvation. Jesus Christ has paid the required price of His own blood to deliver us from satan and sin and to reconcile us to God.

It is God's eternal purpose to redeem humanity through the Person and work of Jesus Christ and to exalt Jesus Christ as Lord over all the nations. That is what God is actively working to accomplish through His prayer partners.

The apostle Paul wrote, "Therefore God also has highly exalted Him [Jesus Christ] and given Him the name which is above every name, that at the name of Jesus every knee should bow, of those in heaven, and of those on earth, and of those under the earth, and that every tongue should confess that Jesus Christ is Lord, to the glory of God the Father" (Phil. 2:9-11).

This redemptive plan and purpose of God has been in His heart in Heaven from eternity past. *The prayer partner He desires is one who understands His plan and purpose and who is willing to co-labor with Him to pray it into a reality on the earth.* Because God is a good God, He answers many of our prayers. But He has bound Himself to answer redemptive prayers because they carry forward His perfect will for mankind.

4

In other words, because God loves us, He delights in answering many of our prayers, even though they do not directly relate to His broader interests. On the other hand, He is obligated to answer redemptive prayers.

The Purpose of Prayer

Everything we do is for a purpose. My wife and I try to walk three miles every morning (groan). This requires a lot of discipline. It would be much easier to sleep late. The flesh loves that!

It's especially difficult for us because we travel a lot and many times it's hard to find a safe place to walk. Somehow, through her basic woman's intuition, Peggy has discovered the safest place to walk in most large cities. It's the mall! It's good for our bodies but not for our finances!

We walk for the purpose of getting exercise. I'm constantly reminding Peggy of our purpose when we are "mall walking." Although it's hard to get our bodies moving, we always feel much better after a vigorous walk.

Prayer also has a purpose. Just like walking, it is a spiritual exercise that requires much discipline. Jesus must have had me in mind when He said, "The spirit indeed is willing, but the flesh is weak" (Matt. 26:41b). I pray early in the morning (before walking). Although it's sometimes hard to get out of bed for that early visit with God, I always feel much better spiritually after a vigorous talk with Him.

The Bible tells us the basic purpose of prayer. It is to glorify God and bring His will from Heaven to earth.

Jesus said to His followers, "And whatever you ask in My name, that I will do, that the Father may be glorified in the Son. If you ask anything in My name, I will do it" (John 14:13-14).

Just as any father desires to be honored by his son, God desires that we honor Him through His only perfect Son, Jesus Christ. We honor God by honoring Jesus Christ.

Jesus Himself said, "That all should honor the Son just as they honor the Father. He who does not honor the Son does not honor the Father who sent Him" (John 5:23).

The way we honor Jesus, and thus God, is by allowing Him to be Lord of our life. When He is fully Lord of our life, our prayers will be focused on Him rather than on ourselves. We will be seeking to do His thing rather than our thing. Then our prayers will be supernatural.

This brings us to the second purpose of prayer, which is to bring God's will from Heaven to earth. God has a will or plan for humanity in general and for our lives individually. The Bible uses various phrases to state this, such as "God's counsel, God's purpose,

God's decree," etc. (See Isa. 46:8-10; Eph. 1:11; Dan. 4:35.)

All of these references tell us that God, out of His own absolute free will, without consulting anyone, has determined to bring about something through His creation according to His own good pleasure. In other words, God decided to do something just because He wanted to do something. He didn't need to; He chose to because it was His good pleasure.

God's "something" is His will for humanity in general and our lives specifically. Do you know that God has a will for your life? He sure does! He wants you to discover the "God something" (both the general and the personal), and pray it into existence on the earth. Wow! Can you think of anything more exciting than that?

It is imperative that we have this divine perspective of prayer. Without it, our prayers quickly become nothing more than pitiful pleas to God to meet our every selfish desire—like children in the candy store begging their parents for goodies.

The Importance of Prayer

This section should help us understand just how important prayer is to God. In fact, it is so important that God has given us His personal phone number. Did you know that God has a phone number? He's even listed it. Many people have an unlisted phone

7

number, but not God. He so wants us to call Him that He has given His number to everybody.

You won't find God's number in a regular phone directory, however. Nor is it listed in the Yellow Pages. You'll find His number in the "Holy Pages" of His sacred phone book—the Bible. *His number is Jeremiah 33:3!*

God gave His phone number to one of His prophets named Jeremiah. Jeremiah was in prison at the time and really needed encouragement from God. Maybe that is why God gave it to him.

God's word to Jeremiah and to us is, "Call to Me, and I will answer you, and show you great and mighty things, which you do not know" (Jer. 33:3).

God wants us to call Him just as all loving parents want their children to call them.

I remember when Mom and Dad first sent me off to camp. It was harder on them than it was on me. It was their first real test to see if their parental training would pay off. Would I remember anything they taught me? Would I embarrass the family? Would I get hurt?

There were the last-minute instructions. Don't talk ugly! Flush the toilet! Say "please" and "thank you." But the very last thing they said, as they waved goodbye, was, "Call us when you get to camp."

Now I had every intention of calling them. But when I arrived at camp, I got so excited with exploring, catching frogs and making new friends that I forgot about calling Mom and Dad. They had to call me!

Aren't we like this with God? He is our loving heavenly Father who desires us to keep in regular touch with Him. But we get so busy exploring this wonderful planet, making a living, meeting people, and sometimes just surviving, that we forget to pray.

Because He loves us, He'll sometimes call us to make sure we're okay! Perhaps this book is a loving call from God to remind you that He desires to hear from you more often.

A number of years ago I got a cordless telephone, but I had to take it back because it didn't work. I've since replaced it with one that I could use without needing a degree in electrical engineering.

God has a cordless telephone called prayer. His phone always works, and you don't have to be a genius to use it.

Sometimes when we try to call another person, there is no answer at the other end of the line. At other times the line is busy. This can be frustrating, particularly when you really need to talk to the person. But nothing can be more annoying than answering machines. I hate talking to answering machines, don't you?

There are other phone features such as call forwarding and call waiting. With call forwarding, you can program your phone to ring in someone else's house. This is a fun trick to play on callers. They think they're calling you, but they're really calling someone else, such as their bill collector. With call waiting, you can program your phone to let you know you're getting an incoming call while you're talking to someone else. This is a good excuse to hang up on the person you're talking to if you don't want to talk to him.

Soon, in one of the most significant advances for telephone customers since touch-tone dialing, you will be able to dial a telephone number by speaking the name of the person you are calling. This is appropriately called voice dialing. You compile a separate voice directory of people's names and simply say the person's name stored in the directory. The phone automatically does the dialing.

Along with the voice dialing, we also have picture phones. With picture phones, you can see the person while you talk to him. That should be interesting. We'll no longer be limited to hearing the person's voice; we'll be able to see the individual as well. Just think, if your picture phone rings, and you answer it while you're raiding the refrigerator, the caller will know exactly what you're doing.

Human telephone systems are becoming very complicated. God's prayer telephone system is certainly easier to use than those of AT&T, MCI, Sprint, etc. When you call God, He will always answer. He's always there to take your call. And He's never too busy running the universe that you can't get through to Him.

Nor will His heavenly phone ring in the angel Gabriel's house. God doesn't have call forwarding or call waiting. He won't put you on hold or hang up on you.

And, you know, God has had voice dialing for 2,000 years. Just mention the name of Jesus and the Holy Spirit will promptly put your call through to God.

God also has a picture phone. When you call Him, the same Holy Spirit who put through your call will give you a vision of God. You'll see Him high and lifted up in His majesty and splendor. You'll look upon His blazing glory and dazzling beauty. The awesome awareness of being in His presence will thrill you beyond words. You'll come to know Him with an intimacy you never thought possible.

By the way, all of our prayer calls to God are free. Jesus Christ has already paid for the call.

Yes, God desires that we call Him, and He promises to answer. When He answers, He will tell us and show us great and mighty things that have never entered our minds.

Do you know that God has great and mighty things in store for you? He certainly does! You may think you're not too important, but you're important to God. He has a wonderful plan for your life. He wants to make Himself known to you and use you to partner with Him in the greatest of all adventures—working out His plan and purposes for mankind through supernatural prayer and fasting.

But, you know, you won't see the glory of God or discover His plan for your life by watching CNN. You'll discover it by dialing God's number: Jeremiah 33:3.

Partnering with God in prayer is even more exciting when we practice fasting. In the Bible, prayer and fasting are linked together as a way of life.

When Ezra sought God's protection, he fasted and prayed. We read his own words: "So we fasted and entreated our God for this, and He answered our prayer" (Ezra 8:23).

God gave Ezra supernatural protection because he prayed and fasted. This same divine protection is available to us today when we seek God as Ezra did centuries ago.

Here's what some famous people have said about prayer and fasting:

So He Himself [Jesus] often withdrew into the wilderness and prayed.

Luke (Luke 5:16)

Pray without ceasing.

Paul (1 Thessalonians 5:17)

…you do not have because you do not ask.

James (James 4:2)

Prayer is the most important thing in my life. If I should neglect prayer for a single day, I would lose a great deal of the fire of faith.[1]

Martin Luther

12

I fear the prayers of John Knox [Scottish reformer] more than an army of soldiers.[2]

Queen Mary

I have so much to do that I must spend several hours in prayer before I am able to do it.[3]

John Wesley

Every man whose life has counted for the church or for the kingdom of God has been a man of prayer. A prayerless Christian is a powerless Christian.[4]

Billy Graham

Let us also reflect that in the prayers of simple people there is more power and might than that possessed by all the great statesmen or armies of the earth.[5]

Ronald Reagan

The greatest thing anyone can do for God and man is pray. It is not the only thing, but it is the chief thing. The great people of earth are the people who pray. I do not mean those who talk about prayer; nor those who say they believe in prayer; nor yet those who can explain about prayer; but I mean those people who take time to pray.[6]

S.D. Gordan

Fasting helps to express, to deepen, and to confirm the resolution that we are ready to sacrifice anything, to sacrifice ourselves to attain what we seek for the kingdom of God.[7]

Andrew Murray

...consecrate a fast, call a sacred assembly.

Joel (Joel 2:15)

13

Moreover, when you fast, do not be like the hypocrites, with a sad countenance. For they disfigure their faces that they may appear to men to be fasting....

Jesus (Matthew 6:16)

Personal Prayer

Heavenly Father, I thank You for wanting to share Your heart with me as I seek You through prayer and fasting. Reveal Yourself to me and help me to be the kind of prayer partner You desire.

Jesus, I thank You for purchasing my salvation with Your blood. I acknowledge that You are my Lord and Savior, and that through You I can come to God with my sins forgiven.

Holy Spirit, I thank You for Your presence in my life. I submit myself to You and desire Your fellowship and wisdom for supernatural prayer and fasting.

Personal Application

1. Write down your own definition of prayer.

2. Why do you think God has chosen to let us partner with Him in accomplishing His will on the earth?

3. Why do you think prayer is more important to God than it is to us?

4. What is God's basic plan and purpose for mankind?

Resources

1. Eleanor L. Doan, *The Speakers Source Book* (Grand Rapids, Michigan: Zondervan, 1973) p. 192.

2. Herbert Lockyer, *All the Prayers of the Bible* (Grand Rapids, Michigan: Zondervan, 1973) p. 24.

3. Eleanor L. Doan, *The Speakers Source Book* (Grand Rapids, Michigan: Zondervan, 1973) p. 193.

4. Billy Graham, *Peace with God* (New York: Pocket Books, 1975) p. 151.

5. President Ronald Reagan, Address to the Nation, December 10, 1987.

6. S.D. Gordon, *The Rebirth of America* (Valley Forge, Pennsylvania: The Arthur S. DeMoss Foundation, 1986) p. 191.

7. Andrew Murray, *With Christ in the School of Prayer* (Old Tappan, New Jersey: Fleming H. Revell, 1953) p. 74.

2

Elements of Prayer

Just as every telephone is different and has its own number (numeric elements), there are different kinds of prayers and prayer elements. These prayers or prayer elements are: (a) worship; (b) praise; (c) confession; (d) intercession; and (e) petition. These may be separate prayers for a given situation, but each of these five elements should be included in a normal, well-balanced daily prayer. It seems that, from studying the Bible, we should pray them, or dial them, in the order stated above.

Worship

The first prayer element is worship. Worship is giving glory to God for who He is in His very essence and being.

The Bible says, "Give to the LORD the glory due His name; bring an offering, and come before Him. Oh, worship the LORD in the beauty of holiness!" (1 Chron. 16:29).

Our modern English word *worship* comes from an Old English word "worthship." This word basically means to ascribe worth to a person and then adore or exalt the person based on the worth ascribed.

If we ascribe great worth to a person, we will greatly adore that person. If we ascribe little worth to a person, we will give that person little honor.

The Hebrew word for worship in the Old Testament is *shachah.* It is used more than 170 times and means to bow down in homage, or to prostrate oneself as an act of acknowledging the superior worth of another. It is the common term for approaching God in worship.

There are several Greek words for worship in the New Testament. The most commonly used one is *proskuneō.* This word is used more than 50 times and means to come toward to kiss. It is an outward act expressing an inward attitude of humble reverence and love.

A good example of the meaning of the word is found in the Gospel of Luke where Luke tells about a woman who washed the feet of Jesus with her tears, then kissed His feet and anointed them with oil (Luke 7:38).

We learn from this example that worship flows out of a loving, intimate relationship with God through Jesus Christ.

There is none more worthy of our worship than God. He is the supreme "worthy One" in the universe.

The more we know Him, the more we will want to worship Him. Worship, therefore, is a response to our relationship with God.

God made us to be worshipers. It is our nature. If we don't worship God, we will worship someone or something else. Because God is the supreme worthy One, He alone is to be worshiped.

God is worthy of our worship because He is God. However, in order for us to worship God, we must know His nature and character. It's easier for us to observe what God does than it is for us to know Him personally. Therefore, in order to worship God correctly, we must get to know Him.

The best way to get to know God is by reading His autobiography, the Bible. The Bible tells us what God is like. He is the self-existing, uncaused Creator of the universe. He is eternal and infinite in His being. He is awesome in His majesty and unchanging in His character. In His greatness, He is sovereign, all-powerful, all-knowing, and everywhere present. In His character, God is perfectly holy, loving, just and good.

As we get a clearer view of these great attributes of God, our natural response is to present ourselves to Him as an offering of worship and to exalt Him for His greatness and goodness.

To help you know God more intimately, I recommend my book, *What Everyone Needs to Know About God*, which you may order by using the order form in the back of this book.

In general, it seems that the Hebrews worshiped God out of a sense of duty rather than out of a relationship. To most, God was unapproachable. But it is God's desire for us to worship Him out of an intimate relationship of loving reverence and trust.

The relationship that is presented in the Bible is one of a father to his children. Jesus said, "But the hour is coming, and now is, when the true worshipers will worship the Father in spirit and truth; for the Father is seeking such to worship Him" (John 4:23).

It boggles the mind to realize that the great and mighty Creator of the universe wants us to know Him as "Father." *The word Jesus used when He spoke of God as His Father was* **Abba.** This Aramaic word is the equivalent to our English word *Daddy.* You can still hear grown children in the Middle East call their father, "Daddy."

"Daddy" describes a human relationship that is very intimate. A relationship "Daddy" has with his children is one of love, fellowship and protection. We know, of course, that this is not always true with human fathers. Many people have difficulty coming into God's presence with worship, love and trust because of a poor relationship with their earthly father.

God, however, is not like our earthly fathers. God is a perfect heavenly Abba who desires a loving relationship with us. He is not some distant deity who stands apart and aloof from our trials. Nor does He sit sternly in condemnation over us. On the contrary, He completely understands us and is able to fully and completely identify with all of our trials.

Since God made us, He understands our limitations. He is sympathetic to our struggles. He remembers that we are born and shaped in iniquity. He knows that our brief journey on earth is but a fleeting moment in which we constantly war against the attacks of the enemy on our soul.

Abba knows our hearts because He knows our makeup. He was there before we were formed in our mother's womb. Therefore, we can come to Him without pretense, just as we are. He will receive us with compassion, kindness, understanding and affection.

Our heavenly Father is merciful and gracious toward us. He is slow to anger. He is good and ready to forgive. He has plenty of mercy. His lovingkindness is always extended to us.

Our loving God is righteous in all His ways and holy in all His works. Therefore, we can trust Him to always do the right thing by us.

Because God loves us, He must discipline us, but His discipline is always perfectly just. It is always consistent with His character and for our own good. We can trust God to move all events for the purpose of sharing His glory with us. We are the constant object of His love and attention. His concern and care for us is never-ending. His patience, compassion, mercy and understanding are always extended to us. Even though He knows the worst about us, Abba still loves us. We can always expect a warm reception from our loving heavenly Father.

Whatever our situation, we can have a calm assurance that Abba is ours and we are His. And as we get to know Him, His perfect love casts out all fear we may have of Him.

When we meditate upon God's greatness and goodness, our desire is to be in His presence. As we come into His presence and worship Him, our love flows to Him and His to us. We experience a wonderful intimate fellowship with Abba that not only fulfills us, but also changes us into His image as the Holy Spirit manifests God's life to us, in us, and through us.

Worship is not what we do with our lips. Worship is a fellowship with God that transforms our lives so we become like Him. True worship, therefore, is imitating God, just as children imitate their earthly fathers.

This is what the apostle Paul had in mind when he said, "But we all, with unveiled face, beholding as in a mirror the glory of the Lord, are being transformed into the same image from glory to glory, just as by the Spirit of the Lord" (2 Cor. 3:18).

Praise

The second prayer element is praise. Praise is different from worship. Worship pertains to God Himself;

24

praise pertains to what God does. Praise is exalting God for His mighty deeds and works of lovingkindness.

King David was one of the great worshipers and praisers of all time. In fact, he wrote much of the Book of Psalms, which is the praise book of the Bible. Here is just one of his prayers of praise: "I will praise You, O LORD, with my whole heart; I will tell of all Your marvelous works. I will be glad and rejoice in You; I will sing praise to Your name, O Most High" (Ps. 9:1-2).

As we develop an intimate relationship with God, we will not only enjoy His fellowship, we will also experience firsthand His mighty deeds and goodness in our lives.

The greatest thing God has done for us is redeem us from the curse of sin, satan and death. We remember Peter's words quoted in the previous chapter, "Knowing that you were not redeemed with corruptible things, like silver or gold, from your aimless conduct received by tradition from your fathers, but with the precious blood of Christ, as of a lamb without blemish and without spot" (1 Pet. 1:18-19).

The fifth chapter of the Book of Revelation records three prayers of worship and praise to Jesus for who He is and what He has done for us. The first prayer is given by the company of the redeemed. The apostle John wrote, "And they sang a new song, saying: 'You are worthy to take the scroll, and to open its seals; for You were slain, and have redeemed us to God by Your blood out of every tribe and tongue and people and nation, and have made us kings and priests to our God; and we shall reign on the earth' " (5:9-10).

Then all the angels of Heaven began to worship and praise Jesus, saying with a loud voice, "Worthy is the Lamb who was slain to receive power and riches and wisdom, and strength and honor and glory and blessing!" (5:11-12)

Then John heard all of creation exalt Jesus with these words, "Blessing and honor and glory and power be to Him who sits on the throne, and to the Lamb, forever and ever!" (5:13b)

In a wholesome family environment, children love to praise Dad for all the things he does for them. How much more should we, the children of God, praise Him for all that He does for us.

Of course, we do not praise God as a means of manipulating Him to do something for us, as children will sometimes do with their earthly father. Instead we praise God as a natural flow of gratitude from our heart to Him for His goodness to us.

There is tremendous power in praise. Praise helps bring us into the presence of God, lifts our burdens, and gives us victory over satan. For years the most important word in my prayers was *please*. Please, God, do this or that. Somewhere along the way I changed from please to praise. I'm so grateful that I learned to praise the Lord. Next to worship, praising God is the most exhilarating of all human experiences.

As we meditate on God's lovingkindness toward us, praise fills our hearts to an overflowing that we cannot contain. We must express our gratitude with our lips and with our lives given to Him as a living sacrifice of praise.

Worship and praise are linked with fasting. We read in the Book of Acts how God gave supernatural direction: "As they ministered to the Lord and fasted, the Holy Spirit said, 'Now separate to Me Barnabas and Saul for the work to which I have called them.' Then, having fasted and prayed, and laid hands on them, they sent them away" (Acts 13:2-3).

There are different Hebrew words in the Old Testament for our English word *praise*. One of these words is *hallal*. In English it is "hallelujah." It means to praise God with great excitement and enthusiasm, like the football fans do when their favorite team wins the Super Bowl. My, what celebration!

Another word is *shabach*. This word means to praise God with a loud voice or shout, like a victory shout. Surely we can praise God in this way for all He has done for us. The victory shout at the football game should be a whisper compared to our shout to God with the voice of triumph!

A third Hebrew word for praise is *yadah*. It means to praise God with uplifted hands. Our uplifted hands represent our whole body, soul and spirit being offered to God as a living sacrifice of praise.

Another Hebrew word translated as praise is *towdah*. It means to praise God as an act of faith in anticipation of His meeting your needs. It is praise in advance, knowing that God is ready, willing and able to help us.

Zamar is a fifth Hebrew word for praise. It means to praise God with a musical instrument. King David was the greatest psalmist of Israel. He praised God on the harp.

We may or may not be able to play a musical instrument, but we can join with others who are musically gifted in our times of public praise to God.

A sixth Hebrew word for praise is *tehillah*. It means to praise God by singing. God wants us to make a joyful noise to Him by singing His praises.

If you can't carry a tune in a bucket, don't worry. God doesn't mind because the Bible says that God inhabits the praises (*tehillah*) of His people (Ps. 22:3 KJV).

A final praise word, and one of the most interesting in the Old Testament, is *barak*. It means to bless God by kneeling or bowing before Him. To bless the Lord means to praise Him for all He has done for us.

Confession

The third prayer element is confession. Confession is agreeing with God concerning our sins. Humans are a lot better at confessing other people's sins than their own.

I have such a great respect for King David. He was literally the most powerful ruler of his time, yet when confronted with his sin against Uriah and Bathsheba, he acknowledged his failure.

Here is his prayer of confession to God: "I acknowledged my sin to You, and my iniquity I have not hidden. I said, 'I will confess my transgressions to the LORD,' and You forgave the iniquity of my sin. Selah" (Ps. 32:5).

In David's prayer of confession, he used the word *my* four times. In other words, he held himself accountable for his actions. He humbled himself before God and acknowledged personal responsibility for his actions rather than blaming Bathsheba or the devil.

Have you ever noticed how people blame things on the devil? Years ago there was a comedian named Flip Wilson who had a well-known television program. He made a fortune blaming things on the devil. His cute little phrase was, "The devil made me do it."

There really is a devil, and he's certainly not our friend. He'll tempt us to sin and do his best to pull us away from God. But he doesn't make us sin. We make our own choices in this life and must accept the responsibility for them. As much as I would like to blame satan for my own failure, I've discovered I can sin real well, even when the devil is out of town.

Children are naturally reluctant to confess their faults to their earthly dads. They are afraid Dad may not understand their situation. Perhaps Dad will punish them or scream at them. Kids are good at making general confessions that don't sound too bad.

We, on the other hand, don't have to fear our heavenly Father in the negative sense of the word. He is not waiting to catch us in the act of doing something wrong so He can hit us with His stone tablets. God understands our failures and loves us. Although we grieve God when we sin, God never gets mad at us. We can come to Him in love and confess our sins.

Our confession to God should be specific. I like to be specific when I'm asking God for help, but not when I'm confessing my sins. Being specific when confessing is shameful and painful. I'd rather be vague and general and let God try to guess which sin I'm confessing. But since God already knows and loves me anyway, I decided a long time ago to "tell it like it is."

The apostle John gives us these words of comfort: "If we confess our sins, He is faithful and just to forgive us our sins and to cleanse us from all unrighteousness" (1 John 1:9).

Incidentally, David was not only one of the great worshipers and praisers of God who confessed his sins, he was also one who practiced fasting as a way of life. Perhaps that is why God said David was a man after His own heart (Acts 13:22).

Intercession

The next prayer element is intercession. Intercession is expressing concern for the glory of God and presenting the needs of others. It is acting as an intermediary between God and man.

Paul wrote the following about intercession: "Therefore I exhort first of all that supplications, prayers, intercessions, and giving of thanks be made for all men" (1 Tim. 2:1).

Intercession is the unselfish element in our prayer. It is seeking God about His purposes on the earth as well as acting on behalf of others.

When I was a child, I often needed an intercessor to plead with Dad not to spank me, even though I deserved it. I feared getting a spanking. Dad would make me get my own switch from the hedge in our yard. If it was not green enough, he would make me get another one. Then I would get a worse spanking.

Dad's spankings hurt. Aren't they supposed to? I would often stuff comic books in the seat of my pants to take the brunt of the switch. I would have used the Sears Catalog, but it was too big to stuff down my pants. By the way, don't ever let your Dad find comic books stuffed in the seat of your pants when he's spanking you.

The only potential intercessor in the house was Mom. I ran crying to Mom pleading for mercy. Mom's intercession kept me from getting a lot of spankings and spared my comic books as well. She not only interceded for me with my earthly Dad, she also talked about me a lot to my heavenly Father. I'm sure her prayers have spared me a lot of spiritual spankings and had much to do with my turning to God later in life.

Because we are naturally self-centered, it is easy to focus our prayers on our own needs. But too much praying for self becomes burdensome. Praying for others not only broadens our participation in God's activities, it also makes our own burdens lighter, can spare our loved ones much heartache, and cause them to turn to God. (I explain this exciting element of prayer more fully in a later chapter.)

Petition

The final element in prayer is our petition to God. It is expressing concern to God for our own needs.

Paul wrote, "Be anxious for nothing, but in everything by prayer and supplication, with thanksgiving, let your requests be made known to God" (Phil. 4:6).

This is one of my favorite verses in the Bible. I guess that's because I have so much I could worry about, if I chose to do so. Wouldn't you be tempted to worry if you did not have a known income?

Peggy and I have not had a known income for many years. As I mentioned previously, when I left my business career I had no bonds to cash, no stocks to sell, no retirement, no insurance, no hospitalization, no savings, no helpers and no church meetings. All I had was God, and He was all I needed. It didn't take me long to learn how to pray.

Living a life of faith, I have never charged a certain amount of money to minister God's Word. I have always operated on the basis of a love offering. I never know if the offering will be big or small. Many times there's more love in the love offering than there is offering.

Personally, we live a very modest life style and do not require much money. Yet my ministry, Sounds of the Trumpet, requires a lot of money.

It would be easy to worry about where the money will come from. But since that's beyond my control, I tell God what I need and let Him worry about it.

Our petitions should be specific. In 1977, my wife required a lot of dental work that cost about $4,000. I didn't have $40, much less $4,000. Where would we ever get that much money? Only God could answer that question! When I asked God to give us money to help us pay the bill, I was startled when He asked me how much I wanted. You see, God wanted me to be specific so when He gave it to me, I would know for sure it was Him.

God miraculously provided the exact amount of money we needed at the time we needed it. He didn't drop it in the backyard—although I had no doubts that He could have if He had chosen to provide it in that manner. However, God usually works in a more conventional way. He uses people. Here's what happened.

Our dentist was very kind and said he would work with us if we needed to borrow the money from the bank. We thanked him but said we would pray and trust God to provide the money. You should have seen the look on his face.

Before Peggy would go to the dentist, we would ask what work he was going to do and exactly how much money we needed for that work. Then we would pray for that exact amount. God provided the money on every occasion.

On one of Peggy's trips, a tooth was to be pulled. I asked God to have the dentist pull the tooth without charging us. When Peggy went to pay for her dental work that day, the bookkeeper said there would be no charge for the tooth that was pulled. Do you know very many dentists who pull teeth for free?

On another occasion, when we asked God to provide the money for the next visit, we thought we needed less than we actually did. So we were somewhat puzzled when God provided more than what we had prayed for. When Peggy went for her dental work, we learned that the dentist planned to do more than we thought. The amount of the bill was exactly what God had sent us. I learned from this experience that God really does know our needs before we ever ask Him (Matt. 6:8).

One of the most interesting miracles relating to this story concerns a stranger who "just happened" to come into our lives when we needed him. In God's providence, He sent a man into our lives who learned of our financial need and asked if he could help. I certainly didn't want to hurt his feelings, so I said, "Yes!" That was the fastest "yes" I've ever gotten out of my mouth.

I had not known this man before, but he gave us $500 a month for five months to help us pay the bill. I saw the man one time after the bill was paid, and I've never seen him again.

God heard our petition and miraculously put this man into our lives for the sole purpose of helping us pay the dentist bill. We didn't have to borrow money or pay the bill over a long period of time. God provided the exact amount we needed at the time we needed it. It didn't come through debt either. It came through supernatural prayer and fasting.

As we live out God's redemptive plan for our life, we are accountable to Him, but He is responsible for meeting our needs. We make known our specific requests and then thank Him in advance for His supply.

Incidentally, not only have I not had a known income for many years, neither have I had any debt. God always pays His bills on time because He doesn't like to pay interest either.

A final thought—when we call someone on the telephone, we normally have a two-way conversation. There are some people, though, who talk so much that it's hard to do much talking ourselves. However, the basic idea is to converse with one another. This means we not only talk, we also listen.

It's the same when we call God on our prayer telephone. If we do all the talking, we'll never hear what He has to say. So we need to be quiet and listen. I've found it helpful to worship and listen, praise and listen, confess and listen, intercede and listen, and petition and listen.

Now that we know God's telephone number, let's offer the following prayer to Him. Then in the next chapter we can learn how to dial His number with confidence.

Personal Prayer

Father God, I worship You for who You are.
You are the self-existing, uncaused Creator of all things.
You are eternal and infinite in all that You are.
I exalt You for Your greatness and goodness.
I acknowledge that You are sovereign, all-powerful,
all-knowing, everywhere present and unchanging.
In Your moral character, You are perfectly holy,
loving, just and good. Father, I praise You
for Your redemptive plan and purposes
for mankind in general and my life specifically.
I desire to be Your prayer partner, helping to bring
Your will from Heaven to earth.

Lord Jesus, I bless You for redeeming me from the curse
of sin, the strongholds of satan, and the fear of death.
Thank You for giving me Your Spirit and new life.

Holy Spirit, I thank You for coming to live in me.
I ask You to reveal the Father's purposes for
my life and help me to glorify Him in my
every word, thought and deed.

Lord, I confess my sins to You and thank You for
forgiving me through the blood of Jesus Christ. I ask
You to create within me a clean heart and renew
a right spirit within me.

Lord, show me those things that are in Your heart
and give me a burden to pray for them. Help me not
to be self-centered in my prayers but to have the
heart of an intercessor.

Finally, Lord, I present my specific requests to You and thank You for hearing my prayer and meeting all of my needs through Jesus Christ my Lord. Amen.

Personal Application

1. Read *What Everyone Needs to Know About God* as a means of developing your sense of worship.

2. Make a list of at least 15 things for which you can praise God.

3. Confess any known sin (be specific) to God and ask Him for revelation of any unknown sin.

4. Ask God to show you for what and for whom He wants you to intercede.

5. Write down your specific needs and ask God to meet them. Thank Him in advance and record the answers in a personal prayer diary.

6. Set a goal to pray at least 15 minutes each day.

3

Praying With Confidence

A deep abiding concern that we all have is whether or not God really will answer our prayers. God certainly wants to answer our prayers, but whether He does or not depends more on us than on Him.

When you call people on your telephone, you don't know if they will answer your call or not. It depends on whether or not they are home and want to talk to you. If you have a close relationship with those people and have their interests at heart, they will talk to you.

You probably have a few close friends who fall into this category. You will always talk to them no matter the time or the circumstances in which they call. That is not true for others whom you do not know personally, or whom you only talk to occasionally.

Similarly, God is always home, and He always wants to talk to you. But His answer depends on your relationship to Him and whether or not you have His interest at heart.

Although God is gracious, and will often help us in our time of need, He is not obligated to answer our prayers if we only know Him casually, talk to Him infrequently, and have little or no knowledge of His plan and purposes. God doesn't like cold calls any more than we do.

You see, prayer is not a crisis hotline on a heavenly 911 that we frantically dial when we are in trouble. *Prayer is a way of life. It flows out of our relationship to God and our concern for His will to be accomplished on the earth.*

God will answer our prayers when we are in right relationship to Him and when our prayers are an expression of His own desires for humanity in general and for our lives specifically. That is what the Psalmist meant when he wrote, "Delight yourself also in the LORD, and He shall give you the desires of your heart" (Ps. 37:4). When we delight ourselves in the Lord, He puts His own desires into our heart and we simply pray them back to Him.

These are the kinds of supernatural prayers we want to learn to pray in this book. So there are six keys that we will now consider.

1. Praying in Faith

The first key is to pray and fast in faith. The writer of the Book of Hebrews makes the following remarkable statement: "But without faith it is impossible to please Him, for he who comes to God must believe that He is, and that He is a rewarder of those who diligently seek Him" (Heb. 11:6).

God wants us to live a life of faith that is based on His promises for our life. What God promises, God provides. When we pray in faith, we are praying in expectation and anticipation of the provision that God has promised. When we diligently seek God in faith, He responds by giving us the provision He promised.

Jesus makes an incredible statement regarding the prayer of faith. He said, "Have faith in God. For assuredly, I say to you, whoever says to this mountain, 'Be removed and be cast into the sea,' and does not doubt in his heart, but believes that those things he says will be done, he will have whatever he says. Therefore I say to you, whatever things you ask when you pray, believe that you receive them, and you will have them" (Mark 11:22b-24).

We learn from these words of Jesus that true faith is not blind faith; it is Bible faith. It is faith in the God of the Bible to answer your prayers.

Jesus boldly declared that God would answer "whatever things you ask." But He was clear in pointing out that our asking must be without doubt and from the heart. The only way we can pray the prayer of faith from our heart, without doubting, is by God Himself putting the faith in our heart.

The kind of faith Jesus is talking about is a supernatural faith that comes from God (1 Cor. 12:9). It doesn't take a lot of that faith to help us pray the prayer of faith. *You see, it's not the amount of faith that matters, but the source of it.*

In another place in the Bible, Matthew records this same teaching from Jesus about mountain-moving faith. Jesus said, "..if you have faith as a mustard seed, you will say to this mountain, 'Move from here to there,' and it will move; and nothing will be impossible for you" (Matt. 17:20).

Jesus used a figure of speech comparing faith to a mustard seed. The mustard seed is very small. What Jesus wanted us to know is that it doesn't take "huge" faith to get our prayers answered. Real faith is supernatural and comes from God. Therefore, it only takes a seed of His faith planted in our heart to pray the prayer of faith. We don't need "more" faith; we need "God's" faith!

The prayer of faith is not some vain repetition or confession of a supposed formula for getting things from God. Neither is it to be confused with our feelings and emotions. The prayer of faith is simply an inward assurance and confidence that God has already made provision for your need and will supply the provision when it is required.

The question we should ask is not "How do I get more faith?" but "How do I get the supernatural, God-kind of faith?"

The apostle Paul gives us the answer. He wrote, "So then faith comes by hearing, and hearing by the word of God" (Rom. 10:17). Faith comes by hearing the Word of God. But this is not just hearing with our physical ears; it is hearing with our spiritual ears.

The New Testament was written in Greek. The Greek language has two words for our one English word. These are *logos* and *rhema*. The *logos* refers to a general word that is written for everyone. The Bible is the *logos* of God. It is God's general word for all of us to read and study. The *rhema* is a spoken word that is specific and personal. It is not for everyone; it's to an individual.

*When Paul said faith comes by hearing and hearing by the Word of God, he used the word **rhema**. This means that God Himself plants supernatural faith in our heart by speaking to us a specific personal word—a **rhema**.*

God normally does not speak this word to us audibly, but by the Holy Spirit giving an inner witness or knowing to our heart that we have received a personal word from God. When God gives us this inner knowing, He plants His own supernatural faith in our heart, enabling us to believe Him. Paul explains this process in Romans 12:3 by saying that God gives each of us a measure of faith in order to believe His promises and to serve Him effectively.

It is important to understand that our believing must come from our heart, not just our head. Many people believe they do act in faith—yet, the promise they are believing God for often does not come. Naturally

45

this leaves the person confused and disappointed. When this happens, they often blame God for not answering their prayer. Instead it may be unanswered because they believed with their mind a general promise (*logos*) that never got in their heart (*rhema*). They act out of presumption rather than from real Bible faith.

The same God who helped people in Bible times pray the prayer of faith, helps us pray with supernatural faith today. Just think, we can partner with God to supernaturally pray Heaven to earth! Here's an example of how it works.

I mentioned earlier that when I left my successful business career, I had no money and no idea where I would ever get another penny. Yet, like everyone else, I had bills to pay. This new life of dependence on God was going to be a real learning experience. This was true not only for me, but also for Peggy, who had to not only trust God, but also trust that her husband really had heard from God.

In seeking God regarding our financial dilemma, I found the following promise in the Bible which I claimed for me and Peggy. "But seek first the kingdom of God and His righteousness, and all these things shall be added to you" (Matt. 6:33). God took this general promise (*logos*) and planted in my heart (*rhema*) a seed of His supernatural faith to believe He would provide for our needs. It wasn't long until this faith was tested.

It was Palm Sunday of 1978 when I was putting the final touches on the teaching I was to give that morning at the church services. The title of the Bible lesson was, ironically, "How to Handle Worry." Little did I know how appropriate that lesson would be for Peggy and me beginning that very morning.

I heard her call my name, "Richard." Peggy doesn't normally call me by my name. It's usually "darling"; "honey"; or some other "wifey" term. She only calls me "Richard" when something is wrong. My ears, always sensitive to her voice, noted a distinct sound of fear in her tone.

Peggy had discovered a lump in her breast. This is a fear all women have tucked away in their subconscious mind. How big is the lump? Is it malignant? Is surgery required? How much surgery?

The lump was not the only concern. We had no hospital insurance and no money to pay for medical expenses. Still something had to be done, and quickly. We gave God several days to perform a miracle and dissolve the lump, but that did not happen.

After having a doctor examine the lump, we realized that surgery was our only wise alternative. But how would we pay for it? My concern as a man of God, but also as a husband, was that I had led Peggy into this life of faith with God and now no hospital would even accept her without insurance.

After several days of praying, the Holy Spirit brought to my attention the promise of the provision from

Matthew 6:33. I began to claim this promise and expect the provision. It came in a most unusual way.

I had an aunt who had died about eight months earlier. Aunt Belle had put a small war bond of $2,000 in my mother's name. However, my mother died prior to Aunt Belle's death. My aunt had never married. Peggy and I visited her when we could because we knew she was lonely. Years later, God returned this kindness to us.

Just when we needed God's provision, a cashier's check made payable to me for $2,000 arrived in the mail. Unknown to me, Aunt Belle had put her war bond in my name. We paid the hospital bill in advance, Peggy's lump was benign, and she has not had another one since. Praise God!

I learned a profound truth from this experience—God always makes a provision for us before He makes a promise to us.

Although the doctor had been very positive, he later told us he was afraid the lump was cancerous. All he could say was how "lucky" we were. Every time he said that, Peggy would say, "No, doctor, we were blessed." This happened so many times that I got embarrassed and asked her not to say it again.

A few days later after taking Peggy home from the hospital, I was visiting a friend who was in the same hospital. I "just happened" to meet Peggy's surgeon on the elevator. When he recognized me, he said, "You sure were blessed."

How God works behind the circumstances of life to answer our prayers is beyond our natural reasoning. Some people would call it a coincidence. But it can only be the providence of God responding to the prayer of faith, one of the keys to supernatural prayer and fasting and triumphant living.

2. Praying in Jesus' Name

The second key to supernatural prayer and fasting is to pray in Jesus' name. Jesus Himself gave us the following promise, one that simply overwhelms our natural reasoning. He said, "And whatever you ask in My name, that I will do, that the Father may be glorified in the Son. If you ask anything in My name, I will do it" (John 14:13-14).

Jesus said we should pray in His name because it is through Him that we have access to God. Just prior to making this incredible promise, Jesus said, "I am the way, the truth, and the life. No one comes to the Father except through Me" (John 14:6).

We are able to approach God in prayer because Jesus Christ prepared the way for us. We come to God based on the righteousness of Jesus Christ, not on our own self-righteousness, which is unacceptable to God.

This promise that Jesus makes us is limitless. He says that He will do anything we ask in His name. Yet, even though the promise is limitless, Jesus qualifies it with two conditions. The prayer must be in His name and it must be a prayer that will glorify God.

Have you ever asked God for something and concluded your prayer by saying, "in Jesus' name," yet the prayer was not answered? Millions of Christians around the world offer daily prayers to God in the name of Jesus. Yet many of those prayers are not answered. Perhaps many of your prayers offered in Jesus' name are not answered.

This apparent contradiction between Jesus' promise and the failure of my own prayer life puzzled me for years. I finally asked God why many of my prayers were not answered, even though I concluded them with the phrase, "in Jesus' name."

Here is what God showed me. By seeking God and studying the Scriptures, I discovered that I never really understood what it meant to pray in Jesus' name. I thought it meant just saying His name at the end of the prayer. But God showed me that it meant something entirely different.

In Bible times, a person's name signified or represented the person who bore the name. Even today, when we think of someone's name, we automatically think of the person who bears the name. We think of the individual's personality, nature, authority, character, reputation, abilities, integrity, etc. *The name represents the sum total of the person.* To do something in someone's name is to do it as his representative with his authority, his character, and his purposes and intent in mind. It is to do it as if the other person himself was doing it.

There are many examples of this name representation in the Bible. The Old Testament tells a story of a man named Isaac who had two sons, Esau and Jacob. When Isaac was old, he intended to give his blessing to Esau, his firstborn. However, Jacob deceived his father and got the blessing for himself. (See Gen. 27.)

The name Jacob means "supplanter" (Gen. 25:26). A supplanter is a person who is a deceitful, conniving schemer. Today we would call Jacob a scoundrel. He's the kind of person who would swindle little old ladies out of their inheritances. He's a con artist. You wouldn't buy a used car from him. When you study the life of Jacob in the pages of the Bible, you will discover that he certainly lived up to his name.

Yet, Jacob had an encounter with the living God. God had appeared to Jacob to deal with his weakness of character. Jacob struggled with God through the night until, finally, God had to cripple Jacob to humble him. Afterwards, Jacob walked with a limp.

Jacob had been humbled by God. He was no longer an untrustworthy scoundrel. His character was changed. He was a broken man of humility and integrity. What had been his weakness had now become his strength. God also gave Jacob a new name to go with his new nature. He called him "Israel," which means "one who contends with God" or "prince of God" (Gen. 32).

In the New Testament, Jesus called a man named Simon to be His disciple. The name Simon means "vacillator." He's a person who lacks commitment. He's unsteady. He's fickle. He wavers back and forth like the waves of the ocean. You never know if he will be there to support you when you need him, particularly in a time of difficulty.

As with Jacob, Simon lived up to his name. As long as Jesus was popular and His ministry growing, Simon was a faithful disciple in Jesus' inner circle. But when Jesus was betrayed and arrested, Simon denied he ever knew Jesus (John 18:15-27).

Jesus prophesied to Simon that he would betray Him (John 13:37-38). Yet Jesus also knew that Simon would repent and become the stable, dependable leader of the disciples. Looking ahead to this character transformation, Jesus changed Simon's name to Peter, which means "a stone" (John 1:42). Instead of being a vacillator, Peter would be as steady as a rock.

As I studied these and many other examples in the Bible, I saw the startling truth of what it means to pray in the name of Jesus. It means to pray as Jesus would pray. It means to pray as His representative on the earth, just as if He Himself was praying. It means to pray with His authority, His character, His mind and for His glory. No wonder many of my prayers had not been answered.

To pray in Jesus' name relates to our lives, not our lips. In fact, we do not even have to say "in Jesus' name" to put our prayer in His name. Still, just using His name at the end of our prayer is meaningless unless we are living in His name and all that it represents. It is our lives that pray, not our lips.

We, like Jacob and Simon, must have a transformation of character in order to pray in Jesus' name. We must humble ourselves before God and walk in humility and integrity. We must not waver between serving God and our own selfish interest. We must commit ourselves to the plan and purposes of God and pray for His glory in our lives. Then, and only then, can we pray in Jesus' name. As the prophet said, "For all people walk each in the name of his god, but we will walk in the name of the LORD our God forever and ever" (Mic. 4:5).

So you see, Jesus really meant it when He said we could ask anything in His name. But He knew we could ask in His name only by living in His name. As we live in His name, our prayers will be the kind that He can answer. They will be consistent with His name and character.

Jesus has given us His name. We are called Christians. We are His name bearers, His representatives on the earth. When we live like Christ, we will pray like Christ. When we pray like Christ, we can ask anything and God will answer our prayers through this powerful key to supernatural prayer and fasting and triumphant living.

3. Praying According to God's Will

The next key to supernatural prayer and fasting is to pray according to God's will. The Bible says, "Now this is the confidence that we have in Him, that if we ask anything according to His will, He hears us. And if we know that He hears us, whatever we ask, we know that we have the petitions that we have asked of Him" (1 John 5:14-15).

Have you ever prayed, but lacked confidence that God really heard your prayer? I'm sure we all have felt that way from time to time. But we offered up a prayer to God anyway, hoping that God would answer it. We said "in Jesus' name" at the end of the prayer because it was supposed to make God help us.

That was the way I prayed for years. To me, prayer was a means God had given me to get my way rather than His way. I was praying "my will be done" rather than "Thy will be done." I thought I could use the name of Jesus at the end of my prayer like a magic wand that would somehow cause the answer to appear. I was so ignorant of the true meaning and purpose of prayer.

John says the way to pray supernaturally with confidence is to pray according to God's will. *True prayer, therefore, is not asking what I want, but what God wants*. It is not convincing God to do something for my benefit and comfort; it is bending my will to His.

In previous chapters, I pointed out that God has a will for mankind in general and for our lives specifically. I mentioned that God desires us to discover His will and partner with Him to pray it from Heaven to earth. As we discover God's will and come into agreement with it, we can pray with boldness, confidence and faith that God will answer our prayers.

The question we should ask ourselves is not "How can I get God to answer my prayers?" Instead we ask, "How can I know God's will?" When we know God's will, and pray according to His will, He promises to answer our prayers.

Many Christians pray with, "if it be Thy will." This sounds very spiritual and certainly appears to be a humble way to pray. However, it is not how the Bible says we should pray. We cannot pray with confidence if we are not sure our prayer is in God's will. We don't know if He will answer it or not. Rather than praying, "if it be Thy will," God wants us to know His will and pray, "Thy will be done on earth as it is in heaven" (see Matt. 6:10).

Yes, we can know God's will for mankind in general and for our lives personally. The writer of Proverbs says, "Trust in the LORD with all your heart, and lean not on your own understanding; in all your ways acknowledge Him, and He shall direct your paths" (Prov. 3:5-6).

The apostle Paul wrote, "I beseech you therefore, brethren, by the mercies of God, that you present your bodies a living sacrifice, holy, acceptable to God, which is your reasonable service. And do not be conformed to this world, but be transformed by the renewing of your mind, that you may prove what is that good and acceptable and perfect will of God" (Rom. 12:1-2).

55

God reveals His will to us in several ways. The most important way is through the Bible. The Psalmist wrote, "Your word is a lamp to my feet and a light to my path" (Ps. 119:105).

God has revealed in His Word almost everything you need to know about His will. He has given principles in the Bible that express His will for all areas of our life. Approximately 90 percent of all guidance you will ever need from God concerning His will comes from the Bible.

Obviously, then, the best way to know God's will is to develop a habit of studying the Bible. To help you understand the Bible, I recommend my book *Come and Dine*, which you may order by using the order form in the back of this book.

Another primary way God reveals His will to us is through the inner voice of the Spirit of God. Jesus said, "But the Helper, the Holy Spirit, whom the Father will send in My name, He will teach you all things..." (John 14:26; also see John 16:13-15).

The Holy Spirit often gives us insight into God's will as we are praying. In fact, we should ask God to reveal His will to us while we pray. We should then listen for God to speak to us. God's Word says, "If any of you lacks wisdom, let him ask of God, who gives to all liberally and without reproach, and it will be given to him" (James 1:5).

I'll never forget a dilemma Peggy and I faced when my grandmother died. I was close to her and felt a great loss at her death. She lived in Tennessee, but was to be buried in Louisiana. I live in Texas.

Unfortunately, the funeral was to be held on the same day we had scheduled a Christian gathering in our home in Houston. We had told many people about the meeting and had invited guest speakers and singers. It was impossible to cancel the meeting, but we also wanted to go to the funeral, which was a five-hour drive from Houston. Naturally, the family would expect us there and certainly wouldn't understand if we were not present.

I didn't know what to do, but I asked God for wisdom. The Holy Spirit spoke to me from God's Word, "Let the dead bury the dead, but you go and preach the kingdom of God" (see Luke 9:60). I had my answer and could act accordingly.

Another important way God reveals His will to us is through divine providence or circumstances. One of the best illustrations in the Bible of this method relates to the story of Joseph.

Joseph's brothers sold him as a slave to the Egyptians. However, God had other purposes for Joseph and made him Prime Minister of Egypt. Joseph held this position during the time of a great famine. Joseph was able to save Egypt and his family by collecting and storing food prior to the famine. (See Gen. 37–45.)

When Joseph finally revealed his identity to his brothers, he said, "And God sent me before you to preserve a posterity for you in the earth, and to save your lives by a great deliverance" (Gen. 45:7).

God was working behind the scenes to bring about His will for Joseph and his family. He'll do the same in your life as well.

Although none of us are perfect and don't always know what is right, if we really want to know God's will and are committed to doing it, God will be faithful to reveal it to us so we can declare it on the earth. We pray and live according to God's will, a necessary key to supernatural prayer and fasting and triumphant living.

4. Praying With a Holy Life

This brings us to the next key to supernatural prayer and fasting, which is to pray with a holy life. Jesus said, "If you abide in Me, and My words abide in you, you will ask what you desire, and it shall be done for you" (John 15:7).

Once again Jesus makes the incredible "ask what you desire" promise regarding prayer. But as with the others, it is conditional. The conditions He mentions are our abiding in Him and His words abiding in us.

What does it mean to abide in Christ? Basically it means to pray and live according to God's will with His life working in us through the active administration of the Holy Spirit. The Holy Spirit reveals God's will to us and manifests His life in and through us.

That is what the apostle Paul meant when he wrote, "...work out your own salvation with fear and trembling; for it is God who works in you both to will and to do for His good pleasure" (Phil. 2:12-13).

The word *abide* means "to have a continuing dwelling or residing relationship with another person or object." Jesus used the word as a figure of speech to illustrate the ongoing relationship He desires to have with us.

The illustration He used was that of a vine and a branch. The vine and the branch have a living union with each other. The vine is the source of life for the branch. It sends its life-giving sap to the branch. The branch has no life in itself. It simply abides in the vine. It is the life from the vine (not the branch) that produces the beautiful flower or fruit. The branch does not produce the fruit. It simply bears the fruit produced by the life-giving sap flowing from the vine through the branch.

As long as the branch abides in the vine and is carefully pruned, it will bear much fruit. Pruning is necessary in order to have a healthy vine. Anything that hinders the vine from producing more fruit should be cut off to allow further growth.

We learn from this illustration that to abide in Christ simply means to live in a daily relationship with Him so His life is continually flowing to and through us. Like the branch, we acknowledge that we have no ability to produce godly fruit within ourselves, but must rely totally on the Holy Spirit to do it for us.

We are also willing to allow God to prune us by removing anything in our lives that would keep us from bearing more spiritual fruit. The more He prunes, the more fruit we will bear.

We see from this illustration that Christianity is a life style. It is not a religion. It is a relationship with Jesus Christ that we can have by yielding ourselves to the Holy Spirit who will reveal God's will to us and produce His life in us.

The second condition Jesus gives is that His words must abide in us. When we fully grasp what Jesus means by this condition, our lives will be radically changed.

Earlier in this chapter I explained the difference between the *logos* and *rhema* of God. You recall that the *logos* of God is the general written Word of God for all of us. The *rhema* of God is the spoken word of God to each of us personally. The word Jesus used for His words "abiding in us" was *rhema*.

When you meditate on God's written Word, the Holy Spirit will give you a specific word from God that is meant for your personal life. The Holy Spirit will quicken this word to your heart so it will abide inside you.

This living Word of God will permeate your entire being—spirit, soul and body. Your mind will be renewed with the mind of Christ. Your emotions will be transformed by His emotions. Your will is changed and empowered by the Holy Spirit. Finally, your body is used by God to partner with Him in supernatural prayer and fasting for His will to be done in your life. No wonder Jesus made this incredible promise to give us whatever we desire because our desires will actually be His desires planted in us. Praying with a holy life is one of the most important keys to supernatural prayer and fasting and triumphant living.

5. Praying With a Forgiving Heart

The fifth key to supernatural prayer and fasting is to pray with a forgiving heart. In the sermon in which Jesus talked about the prayer of faith that would move mountains (Mark 11:23-24), He connected this supernatural kind of praying with forgiveness.

Here are His words: "And whenever you stand praying, if you have anything against anyone, forgive him, that your Father in heaven may also forgive you your trespasses. But if you do not forgive, neither will your Father in heaven forgive your trespasses" (Mark 11:25-26).

As we journey through this life, people will say and do things that will hurt us. Sometimes they do it intentionally and other times they are not even aware that their words or actions affect us. As long as we live on this planet, we will have situations develop that strain our relationship with others.

These situations can either make us bitter or better. They will make us bitter if we harbor resentment in our heart. They will make us better if we forgive.

When we hold a grudge against people, it doesn't hurt them; it hurts us. The people who offended us may not even be aware that they did or said something that upset us. We think that we are hurting them by our resentment. This action makes us feel good because we believe we are getting even.

We are not getting even, however; we are getting bitter. The Bible tells us to make peace with those who have offended us and warns us against the root of bitterness that grows out of the soil of an unforgiving spirit. Bitterness affects not only our relationships with others, but also our relationship with God.

Therefore, the writer of the Book of Hebrews says, "Pursue peace with all people, and holiness, without which no one will see the Lord: looking carefully lest anyone fall short of the grace of God; lest any root of bitterness springing up cause trouble, and by this many become defiled" (Heb. 12:14-15).

The writer then uses Esau as an example of a person who lost God's blessing in his life because he was bitter against his brother (Jacob). Jacob was that scoundrel who cheated Esau out of his birthright. Esau became so bitter that he was unable to forgive Jacob. He lamented his situation, but he did not forgive (Heb. 12:16-17).

If we allow a root of bitterness to grow in our life, it will quickly take over our entire being and choke our ability to be blessed by God and to pray supernatural prayers. *The only way to get rid of the root of bitterness is to forgive those who have offended us.*

This is so important that even Jesus often spoke about it. On one occasion He said, "Therefore if you bring your gift to the altar, and there remember that your brother has something against you, leave your gift there before the altar, and go your way. First be reconciled to your brother, and then come and offer your gift" (Matt. 5:23-24).

The gift Jesus is talking about is the Old Testament trespass offering described in the Book of Leviticus (Lev. 5:14-19; 7:1-10).

God instructed His people to bring a trespass offering to Him whenever they did something that offended Him or someone else. Along with the offering, they were to make restitution for any harm they might have done to a fellow Hebrew. This included reimbursing the offended person in full and adding 20 percent to the value of the loss incurred. This brought about reconciliation between the two people and with God.

Sometimes people would bring their trespass offering to God expecting Him to bless them, but they did not make things right with the one they had offended. Jesus spoke to this situation and reminded them that

God would not accept their gift unless they first reconciled their differences (Matt. 5:23-24).

The same is true for our lives today. We may offer our gift of prayer to God, but He will not bless us with a supernatural answer when we do not forgive those who have harmed us or do not seek forgiveness from those we have harmed.

The apostle Paul exhorts us with these words: "Let all bitterness, wrath, anger, clamor, and evil speaking be put away from you, with all malice. And be kind to one another, tenderhearted, forgiving one another, even as God in Christ forgave you" (Eph. 4:31-32).

When seeking God's help in forgiving those who have disappointed me, I learned a shocking truth: Only God has a right to be angry. Only God has never done anything unrighteous toward anybody, yet He has chosen to forgive us.

If you've never hurt or disappointed anyone, then you have a right to be angry. You have a right to your grudge. But, of course, none of us can say that we never acted in an unrighteous way toward another. None of us can say that we never disappointed another. None of us can say that we don't need forgiveness from someone.

Since God, who alone has the right to be angry with us, has chosen to forgive us, how much more should we, who have no right to be angry, choose to forgive!

Yes, we have many opportunities to practice forgiveness. For the glory of God and our own well-being, we must choose to use these opportunities to make us better, not bitter. Praying with a forgiving spirit is a required key to supernatural prayer and fasting and triumphant living.

6. Praying With Persistence

The last key is praying with persistence. The apostle Paul gives us this key. He says we should be "praying always with all prayer and supplication in the Spirit, being watchful to this end with all perseverance and supplication for all the saints" (Eph. 6:18).

The important word Paul uses in this verse regarding this final key is the word *perseverance*. We must persevere in our prayer life. We must never give up! Once we know we are praying according to God's will, we must be steadfast until we see the answer manifested.

Years ago when God directed me to leave my career, I was praying and fasting for specific direction regarding His will for my life. I believed He wanted me to write Christian books. Because this was to be such a dramatic change in my life, I asked God to confirm what I was thinking. He did this in several ways. One was so clear that I knew God had answered my prayer.

Here's what happened. I picked up a book by Frances Roberts, entitled *On the Highroad of Surrender*

65

(King's Farspan, Inc., 1973). As I looked at the Table of Contents, my eyes seemed to be drawn to a specific inspirational topic. It was called, "My Words Cannot Wait." I turned to page 38 and read the following words, which I am quoting with permission from the publisher.

The hour is late, and the time for ministering is limited. Delay not, but hasten to finish the work. I have other work for you, and it waits only the completion of the present task. Do that which is nearest at hand. I shall open a way for its fulfillment, so you need not hold back, wondering how the provisions will be supplied. Lacked you ever in the present? Have you not acted in each case with faith in Me as your only hope? Yes, child, I say to you, walk on. There are no limits to the promises of God.

My words cannot wait; but you have held them as though you thought the future would wait. Up! Delay no more. Obey Me, and do so quickly. There is a door open that may soon be shut. There are hearts ready that will be turned in discouragement to error but for your words. Send forth the message and trust Me with its end. I hold all things in My power, and I shall direct its goings. Do not analyze the situation, nor seek to protect yourself from misunderstanding nor My words from rejection.

Lo, the Spirit accompanies the word, and you may know and be confident that My Spirit anointing the page will bring light and revelation and the confession that God has truly spoken. Yield and labor. I will add

*the blessing and the reward. I have called you by name.
I have given you My words, and I will not have them set
aside either by you or by others.*

*Renew your faith. Look directly to Me. I will em-
power and I will make all things possible as you move in
obedience.*

Wow! What an answer from God. As inexperienced
as I was at hearing from God, even I knew He had spoken. So I began to write my manuscripts.

Because of the urging of that guidance, I thought
the books would be quickly published and distributed
around the world.

I was on fire for God but very naive. I thought the
Christian publishing companies would surely be knocking on my door begging for my manuscripts. After all,
hadn't God told me to do this? I was certainly in for a
big surprise.

I had no idea how to get a book published. I began
by sending inquiry letters to every Christian publishing company I knew. I expected the phone to ring any
moment with offers to publish my writings. Instead,
all I received were rejection letters—lots of rejection
letters! Some were not even letters. They were pre-
printed postcards. So much for pride. I got so many I
found myself reluctant to even walk to the mailbox.

That was back in the early 1980's. I felt like giving
up many times. However, we don't live by our feelings.

We live by the *rhema* of God spoken to us in times of prayer and fasting. (See Matt. 4:4.)

It has been a number of years since God gave me that word of confirmation. He has certainly been faithful to bring it to pass. He did get those first books published, as well as many more that have touched the lives of tens of thousands of people around the world. But it didn't happen overnight. It took a lifetime of persistent supernatural prayer and fasting.

Along the way, the devil did everything he could to keep me from getting the job done. There were many difficult trials and much tribulation. Without God's help, the seemingly never-ending challenges, broken promises and disappointments would have overwhelmed me. *Persistent supernatural prayer and fasting was my life line to God that enabled me to overcome them all.*

I can say, along with the apostle Paul, "Now thanks be to God who always leads us in triumph in Christ, and through us diffuses the fragrance of His knowledge in every place" (2 Cor. 2:14).

We'll learn why persistence is necessary in Chapter 5. But for now, I want to end this chapter with a quote from George Mueller. George Mueller was a wonderful man of God who lived in the 1800's. God used him mightily to establish orphanages throughout England.

George Mueller was a great man of prayer who depended wholly on God to meet his needs. In spite of many obstacles, he successfully accomplished the task

God gave him and prayed in over eight million dollars along the way.

George Mueller had the following to say about persistence in prayer. (This quote is taken from a prayer card published by Interdenominational Tract Service.)

When once I am persuaded that a thing is right, I go on praying for it till the end comes. I never give up till the answer comes. The great fault of the children of God is that they do not continue in prayer. They do not persevere. If they desire anything for God's glory, they should pray until they get it.

Personal Prayer

Heavenly Father, I worship You for who You are and praise You for Your great plan of redemption for mankind. I thank You that You have a special plan for my life. I desire to live a holy life that is pleasing to You so You can accomplish Your plan through me.

Lord Jesus, I want to abide in You so Your words may abide in me. I desire to live in Your name as Your representative on the earth. I want to bring glory and honor to Your name by the way I live. As You have forgiven me, help me to forgive and receive forgiveness.

Holy Spirit, I ask You to show me the Father's will for my life. Speak the word of faith to my heart so I might pray without doubting. Give me the strength and courage to be steadfast so I will not waver in accomplishing the tasks You reveal to me.

Lord, I thank You for causing me to triumph over all the roadblocks the devil would put in my path. Thank You for helping me to overcome them all and to faithfully serve you. Thank You for meeting every need in my life and fulfilling the desires of my heart. Amen.

Personal Application

1. Describe how you can receive the faith of God to pray with conviction and assurance.

2. Explain what it means to pray in the name of Jesus.

3. State the three primary ways we discover God's will for our lives.

4. What does the phrase "It is the life that prays" mean?

5. Why is it necessary to pray with a forgiving heart?

6. Explain why it is important to be persistent in prayer.

71

4

Praying Without Hindrances

Reasons Prayers Aren't Answered

The telephone is surely one of the greatest inventions of all time. I still marvel that I can push a few buttons and talk to someone in another location. This ability to communicate long distance has certainly changed our world. But sometimes when we place a call there is static on the line. We can't get through to the other person. So we hang up and try again.

God's prayer telephone is an even greater invention. It staggers the mind to think that we can talk with God. Our ability to communicate with Him through prayer is the means He has given us to change the world. But sometimes when we place our call to God there is static on the line. We can't get through to Him. As we often do with our own telephones, we hang up and try again.

There are many hindrances in our lives that can cause static on our prayer telephone line. In this chapter we will discover eight of them.

1. Wrong Motives

One of the most subtle hindrances is wrong motives. James tells us, "You ask and do not receive, because you ask amiss [wrong motives]..." (James 4:3).

Motives can be subtle because the thing we want is often good, yet we ask for the wrong reason.

A story in the Bible provides a good example. Philip was an evangelist who preached in the city of Samaria. God worked powerful miracles through Philip. Many people were delivered from demons and healed. As a result, the people of Samaria greatly honored Philip.

Now there was a certain man in the city named Simon. Simon was a sorcerer. For many years he was the most powerful man in Samaria. The people revered him.

The miracles God performed through Philip were greater than the miracles the devil performed through Simon. The people honored Philip more than they did Simon. Simon became a believer and was baptized (Acts 8:13). But he was bitter and jealous. He got even angrier when John and Peter arrived in Samaria and God worked miracles through them too.

Simon was losing his prestige and his business. In desperation, he offered them money, thinking he could buy the power of God and use it for his own selfish purposes.

The disciples sternly rebuked Simon. Peter said to him, "Your money perish with you, because you thought that the gift of God could be purchased with money! You have neither part nor portion in this matter, for your heart is not right in the sight of God" (Acts 8:20-21).

Simon wanted a good thing, but he wanted it for the wrong reasons. His heart was not right in the sight of God.

I heard a minister tell a story about himself that was similar to Simon's story. He said that God had worked great miracles through him at one time, but the miracles had ceased. When he asked God about it, God answered him in a dream.

In his dream, God told the minister to go to a certain house in his city and pray for a woman who was near death. The minister was not to tell the sick woman his name. He was to anoint her with oil, pray the prayer of faith for healing, and then leave. As the minister prayed for the woman, God instantly healed her. He then left the house, as God had instructed him.

About that time, the dream ended and the minister awakened in a fit of anger against God. He was angry because God wouldn't let him tell the sick woman his name so she could praise him. He wasn't grateful to God, nor was he concerned about the woman. He was concerned only about his own reputation. When the minister realized that, he repented and God once again worked miracles through him.

The minister was like Simon. He wanted something good, but for the wrong reason. That was the static on his prayer telephone line. It was a bad connection keeping him from receiving the power of God.

If our prayers are not being answered, we should ask God to show us the motives in our heart. King David did the same with these words: "Search me, O God, and know my heart: try me, and know my thoughts: and see if there be any wicked way in me, and lead me in the way everlasting" (Ps. 139:23-24 KJV).

2. Sin

Sin is another cause of static on our prayer telephone line. Isaiah instructs us with the following hard, but necessary, warning: "Behold, the LORD'S hand is not shortened, that it cannot save; nor His ear heavy, that it cannot hear. But your iniquities have separated you from your God; and your sins have hidden His face from you, so that He will not hear" (Isa. 59:1-2).

God is a good God and desires to help us. He wants to answer our prayers. However, our sin can hinder Him from doing so.

A story in the Bible that dramatically illustrates this point is found in the Book of Joshua. God promised to give the land of Canaan to the children of Israel. He promised to help them defeat their enemies and take their cities.

Their first battle was for the city of Jericho. Because it would be their first victory, God told the Hebrews not to take any treasure for themselves. They were to give it to God as a first-fruits offering. Joshua led the people to victory just as God had promised.

In spite of God's clear instructions, a man named Achan took some silver and gold for himself. He hid it so no one would find it.

The next city to be taken was Ai. This was a small city. The Hebrews should have easily conquered it. Instead, they were soundly defeated.

Joshua was shocked by the defeat. Hadn't God promised him victory? What went wrong? Had God changed His mind? Had God forsaken them? I'm sure these and many other questions raced through Joshua's mind.

When Joshua asked God for an explanation, God told him what Achan had done and that his disobedience was the reason they were defeated. Achan's secret sin caused their defeat. When Achan was exposed, and the people repented, God gave them a great victory at Ai. (See Josh. 6–7.)

The tragic story of Achan is an example from which we can learn. God has promised to give us victory over the enemies of our soul. But as Achan robbed God, our secret sin can rob us of the victories God has for us. Like the static on the line, sin can interfere with our communications with God.

The Psalmist warns us against secret sin but encourages us to expect God to answer when we forsake that sin. He writes, "If I regard [hold on to] iniquity in my heart, the Lord will not hear. But certainly God has heard me; He has attended to the voice of my prayer. Blessed be God, who has not turned away my prayer, nor His mercy from me!" (Ps. 66:18-20)

3. Unforgiveness

A third hindrance to answered prayer, one which we have already discussed, is unforgiveness. We must have a forgiving heart if we seriously desire God to answer our prayers. Unforgiveness can perhaps cause more static on our prayer telephone line than anything else.

God answers our prayers primarily on the basis of our sins having been forgiven. However, He cannot communicate with us on the basis of forgiveness if we do not forgive others. *Our unforgiveness of others blocks the flow of God's forgiveness to us.*

Jesus spoke very bluntly about the absolute necessity of forgiveness. He said, "For if you forgive men their trespasses, your heavenly Father will also forgive you. But if you do not forgive men their trespasses, neither will your Father forgive your trespasses" (Matt. 6:14-15).

On another occasion, Jesus told a story to illustrate the tragic consequences we might experience in life if we refuse to forgive. He said a king decided to settle accounts with his servants. One servant owed the king a huge sum of money, but was unable to repay the king. The king commanded that the servant and his family be sold, along with all of his possessions, and the money be given to the king for repayment. The servant begged the king to give him more time to repay the debt. The king showed mercy to the servant and forgave him his large debt.

The forgiven servant then went to one of his fellow servants who owed him a very small amount of money. He demanded instant payment. When the fellow servant could not repay the debt, the forgiven servant had the man put in prison.

When the king learned what the forgiven servant had done, he got very angry. He summoned the forgiven servant and punished him until he paid all that he owed the king. (See Matt. 18:23-35.)

The story clearly illustrates the importance of forgiveness. The first servant received mercy and was forgiven a large debt. Yet he showed no mercy to another servant who owed him a small debt. He had been forgiven himself, but he refused to forgive another.

God has forgiven us the great debt of sin. Since He has forgiven us such a large debt, we certainly should forgive others the relatively small debt they owe us.

A number of years ago when I gave this teaching in a Bible class, a young woman told me how she experienced this truth in her own life.

She was a Christian and had been blessed by God with a beautiful singing voice. For years she begged God to open doors for her to minister in song. She wanted to use her talent for God's glory. But all the ministry doors she tried to open were locked.

When she heard me give this teaching, the Holy Spirit reminded her of an unforgiving spirit she had against someone who had offended her in the past. Later that day she called the person long distance and forgave that individual for the offense. The very next day, she received a telephone call from a Christian television station asking her to sing on one of their programs.

4. Marital Conflicts

One of the most common, but overlooked, hindrances to answered prayer is marital difficulties. If you are single, you might think you can relax because this one doesn't apply to you. However, this could be the reason you are single. So whether you're single or married, don't skip this one.

The apostle Peter gives us some very important instructions on how wives and husbands should relate to one another. Contrary to the Catholic inference to Peter's celibacy (as they consider him to be the first pope),

Peter knew what he was talking about because he was a married man (see Mark 1:30).

Peter writes, "Wives, likewise, be submissive to your own husbands, that even if some do not obey the word, they, without a word, may be won by the conduct of their wives, when they observe your chaste conduct accompanied by fear [respect]..Husbands, likewise, dwell with them with understanding, giving honor to the wife, as to the weaker vessel, and as being heirs together of the grace of life, that your prayers may not be hindered" (1 Pet. 3:1-2,7).

Many times husbands and wives do not get their prayers answered because of the way they treat each other. Wrong relationships between husbands and wives cause a lot of interference on the prayer telephone line. However, we can clear the line by following Peter's instructions.

The word he gives to wives is, "Be submissive to your own husbands." I doubt if there is any word in the English Bible more misunderstood than the word *submissive.* Men have used this word as a club to beat women over the head for centuries. However, this word means something totally different than what most people think.

To understand what submission means, we must relate it to another word: *obedience.* This is important because most people confuse these two words. They think submission and obedience are the same. They are not the same!

Obedience is an outward action. Submission is an attitude of the heart. God never expects us to obey an ungodly command from anyone (see Acts 5:29). But He does expect us to have a humble and gentle spirit, even if we are forced to rebel.

Peter does not tell the wife to obey her husband. He tells her to have a gentle and quiet spirit. Husbands and wives should be in agreement with one another. However, if a husband tells his wife to do something (obey) that is against God's Word or her conscience, she must refuse (disobey). What matters is her attitude. Rather than being arrogant and haughty, she should respond in a quiet, respectful, courteous manner. Of course, this is easier said than done. But the Holy Spirit will help the wife develop this attitude.

Many Christian women spend long hours praying about the spiritual condition of their husbands. They want their husbands to be saved or to be more Christlike, and to take the spiritual leadership in the marriage. However, her own unChristlike disposition may be the very thing keeping her husband from God.

The Christian wife would be wise to remember that her husband is more likely to respond to her actions than he is to her words. If she doesn't like something about her husband, she should tell God about it, not her husband.

The word Peter gives to husbands is to understand and honor the wife as the "weaker vessel" (1 Pet. 3:7).

Paul adds that husbands "ought to love their own wives as their own bodies." (See Eph. 5:28-33.)

Once again, this is easier said than done. But the same Holy Spirit who helps the wife have a godly attitude will also help the husband to love, honor and cherish his wife.

Husbands usually ask God to help them with jobs and financial problems. They want to be successful and make more money. They want their children to behave themselves and their wife to respect them rather than nag them. But, just as with the wife, they can be their own hindrance to their prayers getting answered.

God will not answer the prayers of a man who physically abuses his wife or who seeks to dominate her. He will answer the prayers of a husband who is understanding, tender, caring and affectionate toward his wife and who seeks her best interest as a loving servant-leader.

5. Satanic Resistance

A regular source of interference on our prayer telephone line is satanic resistance. This is a recurring hindrance that Western Christians sometimes fail to recognize. This failure to recognize and take authority over demonic spirits is a major cause of unanswered prayer.

There is a real devil who commands an army of demonic spirits. Satan and his army of demonic spirits actively work to oppose the purposes of God. Their main fear is of prayer because it is through the prayers of God's people that the purposes of God are brought from Heaven to earth. That is why satan will do everything he can to keep you from praying.

We will discuss this subject further in later chapters. At this point, we just need to be aware that satan does fight against our prayers and can delay the answers.

One of the clearest examples of satan's hindering prayer can be found in the Book of Daniel in the Old Testament.

Daniel was a young man who decided that knowing the plan and purposes of God was more important than knowing the names of the players on the Babylonian Super Bowl team. He determined to supernaturally pray and fast for three weeks.

God sent an angel to Daniel with the answer to Daniel's prayer, but satan opposed the angel for the entire three weeks. Finally, God sent Michael the archangel to overpower satan so the first angel could get to Daniel. When the angel arrived, he explained to Daniel the reason for his delay.

Daniel gives us the following personal account: "Then he [the angel] said to me, 'Do not fear, Daniel, for from the first day that you set your heart to understand, and to humble yourself before your God, your words were heard; and I have come because of your words. But the prince of the kingdom of Persia [demon powers] withstood me twenty-one days; and behold, Michael, one of the chief princes [angels], came to help me...' " (Dan. 10:12-13).

I don't know how well you comprehend this story, but it boggles my mind. *Just think, our supernatural prayer and fasting stirs the spirit world to action.* Wow! This is really exciting.

Daniel's prayer was heard the first day he presented it to God. But satan prevented the answer from getting to Daniel until God intervened by sending Michael to end the conflict. This is the ultimate in partnering with God to bring His will from Heaven to earth. This is spiritual warfare at its best. Although the action was in the realm of the heavenlies, it was triggered on earth in the heart of a man who persisted in supernatural prayer and fasting until he received his answer.

Although we cannot see this spiritual battle taking place with our physical eyes, it's just as real as any earthly battle we can see. Such spiritual warfare, then, is one reason our prayers are hindered. But we can overcome this interference on our prayer telephone line by using the authority God has given us in spiritual warfare.

6. Unbelief

Another hindrance to our prayers' being answered is unbelief. In our earlier discussion of the prayer of faith, we read Hebrews 11:6. It would be good to read it again at this time: "But without faith it is impossible to please Him, for he who comes to God must believe that He is, and that He is a rewarder of those who diligently seek Him."

When a human father gives his word to his child, he certainly expects his child to believe he will do what he says. Although human fathers are imperfect and sometimes fail to keep their word, they normally want what is best for their children and will keep their promises, if at all possible.

Our heavenly Father certainly desires the best for His children. He wants us to have an abundant life full of love, joy and peace. He wants us to be free of any destructive habits and tormenting spirits. He wants us to walk in health and prosperity, even as our souls prosper (3 John 2). He wants us to be in right relationship with Him and with one another. He wants us to discover His plan and purposes for our life. He is committed to helping us successfully accomplish His will and will give us whatever we need to serve Him. We are indestructible until we finish the job He has given us.

God has given us His Word. He says to us through the prophet Isaiah, "So shall My word be that goes forth from My mouth; it shall not return to Me void, but it shall accomplish what I please, and it shall prosper in the thing for which I sent it" (Isa. 55:11).

*God's Word (**rhema**) carries within it the life of God Himself. His own life-power accompanies His Word to accomplish His Word in us. The power of His life in His Word will always fulfill the promise of His Word—but we must believe God's Word!*

An unfortunate example of unbelief is the response of the people in Jesus' own hometown of Nazareth. He went to Nazareth to teach. The people marveled at His words, but they did not receive them. The people knew Jesus only as the human son of Mary. They did not recognize Him as the divine Son of God. They saw Him with only their physical eyes, not their spiritual eyes. As a result, their unbelief hindered the Word of God from working miracles among them.

Mark explains, "Now He [Jesus] could do no mighty work there, except that He laid His hands on a few sick people and healed them. And He marveled because of their unbelief..." (Mark 6:5-6).

God wants to do a mighty work in our lives. He wants the life-power of His Word accomplishing Heaven's miracles in us on earth. We must not be like the citizens of Nazareth. We are citizens of Heaven and the Kingdom of God. We need to see Jesus with our spiritual eyes. He is not just a great teacher or nice fellow who went about doing good. He is the exalted Lord of the universe. He can perform His Word!

Because of Jesus Christ's nature, the apostle Paul offered the following prayer on our behalf. It would be helpful to make it your own prayer—just substitute your own name in place of the pronouns.

Paul prayed, "That the God of our Lord Jesus Christ, the Father of glory, may give to you the spirit of wisdom and revelation in the knowledge of Him, the eyes of your understanding being enlightened; that you may know what is the hope of His calling, what are the riches of the glory of His inheritance in the saints, and what is the exceeding greatness of His power toward us who believe, according to the working of His mighty power" (Eph. 1:17-19).

As we think about Paul's prayer, we must understand that God does not reveal Himself to casual inquirers. He speaks His Word to us when we diligently seek Him with our whole heart, fully expecting Him to keep His promises to us.

When we hear God's voice say, "This is the way, walk in it" (see Isa. 30:21), we declare God's Word and then act on it in the faith that comes through supernatural prayer and fasting.

I recall a humorous episode in my life that illustrates this process. A number of years ago I wrote a book entitled, *Radical Christian Living*. I wanted someone to write a foreword for the book. At that time, about the most radical Christian I could think of was Dr. Paul Yonggi Cho. Dr. Cho happens to be the pastor of the largest church in the world in South Korea. I doubt if anyone knows for sure how many members he has in his church. It numbers in the tens of thousands.

I thought it would be nice to have the pastor of the largest church in the world write a foreword to one of my books. I felt led to write him with this request. The only problem was Dr. Cho did not know me. And I had never even been to South Korea. The only thing I knew about South Korea was that it is south of North Korea. Can you imagine the demands on the pastor of the largest church in the world? He probably does not sit around reading letters from someone he doesn't know. However, I sent the letter anyway.

Several days later, I told a friend that Dr. Cho was going to write the foreword to my new book. My friend laughed so hard, I thought he was going to fall off the couch. That was the most absurd comment he had heard in a long time. But I declared it and prayed.

About a month later I received Dr. Cho's foreword in the mail. Guess who was the first person I called? It was my friend. When I told him the news, there was a long period of silence on his end of the telephone line. He just couldn't believe it. That was his problem all right—doubt and unbelief. I sure enjoyed making that call to my friend. I had a good laugh. God is faithful, and we can believe His Word.

7. Disobedience

Disobedience is another source of static on our prayer telephone line. The apostle John writes, "Beloved, if our heart does not condemn us, we have confidence toward God. And whatever we ask we receive from Him, because we keep His commandments and do those things that are pleasing in His sight" (1 John 3:21-22).

It is impossible to pray with confidence when we live in disobedience to God's Word. Our heart condemns us before God, and the last thing we want to do is pray. We know we are out of fellowship with God and really can't expect Him to answer our prayers.

Not only does the Holy Spirit convict us, but satan takes advantage of our broken fellowship with God and condemns us. We feel guilty and, therefore, don't pray with confidence.

When we are living in obedience to God's Word, however, our heart will not condemn us. We will have confidence toward God, fully expecting Him to answer our prayers. God answers our prayers, not as a reward for obedience, but as a result of obedience.

There are many examples in the Bible of people missing the blessings of God because of their disobedience. When God brought the Hebrew people out of Egypt, He promised to give them the land of Canaan. But the people constantly complained as they made their journey to the Promised Land. On ten occasions they disobeyed God (Num. 14:22).

When it came time for the Hebrews to enter the land, God directed Moses to send 12 spies into the land. They stayed in the land 40 days and returned to camp with their report.

Ten of the 12 spies gave a bad report. Instead of believing God to give them the land, they were frightened by the giants and the massive fortified cities. Only Joshua and Caleb gave a good report. They saw the same giants and fortified cities that the other spies did, but believed the promises of God. They encouraged the people to pray and obey.

Unfortunately, the people believed the bad report of the ten spies. They disobeyed God and refused to follow Joshua and Caleb into the land. As God's judgment, they were required to wander in the desert for 40 years (one year for each day the spies were in the land), until the entire rebellious generation of 20 years old and older died. (See Num. 13–14.) Of that generation, only Joshua and Caleb lived to go into the land.

This is such a tragic story. An entire generation died in the wilderness because they disobeyed God's Word. Joshua and Caleb believed and obeyed, and so lived to enjoy the blessings of God in the land.

What a lesson for us today. In fact, the apostle Paul tells us that the things that happened to the Hebrews because of their disobedience are examples we can learn from (1 Cor. 10:11).

God has promised us a wonderful spiritual land full of the milk and honey of His blessings. He has promised to defeat all the spiritual giants and walled cities that we must fight in order to have His blessings.

We must choose which report we will believe and obey. If we choose the bad report of the doubting spies, we will spend our entire Christian life wandering aimlessly in a spiritual desert. If we choose the good report and act in obedience, God will help us defeat our enemies and give us victory. With God's help, let us choose to pray and obey.

8. Praying Against God's Will

The final source of a bad connection on our prayer telephone line is praying against God's will.

We've already discussed the fact that God has a will for mankind in general and for our lives specifically. The Bible verse we read then, which also applies to this discussion, is First John 5:14-15. It says, "Now this is the confidence that we have in Him, that if we ask anything according to His will, He hears us. And if we know that He hears us, whatever we ask, we know that we have the petitions that we have asked of Him."

One point I have tried to stress in this book is that prayer is not a formula. It is a way of life. When we seek an ongoing relationship with God, He will begin to reveal His will to us.

When we first become Christians, we're like babies. Babies are not very interested in their father's will. Babies are interested in getting their own way. They want what they want, when they want it. Babies learn very quickly how to get their own way—they cry a lot. They discover that if they cry, Mom and Dad will come running to meet their every desire.

Babies don't like to be uncomfortable. They don't like to be inconvenienced. They don't like to wait. They learn very early that crying is the formula they can use to manipulate Mom or Dad to give them whatever they want.

However, as the baby grows older, and Mom and Dad wiser, the baby discovers that the formula for manipulating Mom and Dad doesn't work as well as it did when the baby was younger. Mom and Dad don't respond so quickly. They may not respond at all.

Now baby grows a little wiser. Baby realizes that Mom and Dad won't give everything that baby wants. What a shocking revelation for baby. Baby learns he must do what Mom and Dad want him to do, if baby will have his needs met.

As this maturing process continues, baby finally puts away the formula that worked so well in the past. Instead of being a "crybaby," baby seeks to do what pleases Mom and Dad.

In doing so, baby discovers that the natural result of pleasing Mom and Dad is their response of meeting baby's needs and wants whenever possible. This new way to relate to Mom and Dad becomes a way of life for baby. Instead of being self-centered, baby is now Mom-and-Dad-centered. Tears are replaced by a relationship.

This is how our relationship develops with God. If we are baby Christians, we will think of prayer as a means of getting our own way. Because we are self-centered, we try to find just the right prayer formula or confession that will cause God to do what we want Him to do. We become spiritual crybabies. Like the baby who seeks to manipulate Mom and Dad, we seek to manipulate God to do our bidding.

Our heavenly Father is a good God. He will often answer the prayers of baby Christians if the answer does not violate His moral character and is not harmful for us. He does this in His permissive will.

However, God wants us to discover His perfect will. He wants us to be God-centered, not self-centered. He desires that we put away our pleading and tears to get Him to do what we want to make life convenient and comfortable for us. He wants us to be concerned for His will, to bring it from Heaven to earth through an on-going relationship with Him.

After a while, praying against God's will causes so much interference on our prayer telephone line that God, like Mom and Dad with the crying baby, no longer responds. It becomes a hindrance to our prayers getting answered.

As we grow in our relationship with God, our focus is on Him rather than on us. We seek to want to please Him. His desires become our desires. His plans become our plans. His will becomes our will. We bring that will to earth through a life style of supernatural prayer and fasting.

I'm eternally grateful to God that Peggy and I have discovered this for our own lives. He wants you to discover it for your life also. Here are some practical suggestions that have worked for us.

1. Determine in Your Heart to Do God's Will

Jesus was determined to do the Father's will. He said, "For I have come down from heaven, not to do My own will, but the will of Him who sent Me" (John 6:38).

When we are determined to do God's will, He will show it to us. We will know if we are hearing God's voice, our own voice, or the devil's. Jesus promised us this assurance with these words: "If anyone wills to do His will, he shall know concerning the doctrine, whether it is from God or whether I speak on My own authority" (John 7:17).

2. Ask God to Show You His Will

Jesus knew the Father's will. He said, "And this is the will of Him who sent Me, that everyone who sees the Son and believes in Him may have everlasting life; and I will raise him up at the last day" (John 6:40).

We can also know the Father's will. In Chapter 3, I discussed the three primary ways God reveals His will to us. These are studying the Bible, listening to the inner voice of the Holy Spirit, and divine providence. As we seek God in these ways, we can have confidence that God will guide us. The prophet Isaiah declares, "The LORD will guide you continually..." (Isa. 58:11).

James writes, "If any of you lacks wisdom, let him ask of God, who gives to all liberally and without reproach, and it will be given to him. But let him ask in faith, with no doubting, for he who doubts is like a wave of the sea driven and tossed by the wind. For let not that man suppose that he will receive anything from the Lord; he is a double-minded man, unstable in all his ways" (James 1:5-8).

3. Wait Quietly for God's Guidance

Jesus often went into the desert to pray for strength and to seek the Father's will. He would, no doubt, wait on the Holy Spirit for guidance and then go and do what He heard the Spirit say to Him.

Luke writes of Jesus, "So He Himself often withdrew into the wilderness and prayed" (Luke 5:16).

It was in these times of prayer that God the Father spoke to Jesus through the Holy Spirit. Jesus confirmed this by saying, "Most assuredly, I say to you, the Son can do nothing of Himself, but what He sees the Father do; for whatever He does, the Son also does in like manner" (John 5:19).

As we pray in accordance with God's Word, with a pure heart, we ask the Holy Spirit to control our thoughts and reveal God's will to us. This requires us to wait quietly for God to speak to us.

A good example in the Bible is the Old Testament prophet Habakkuk. He prayed to God and then waited for God's answer. He said, "I will stand my watch and set myself on the rampart, and watch to see what He will say to me...Then the LORD answered me and said..." (Hab. 2:1-2).

The Bible encourages us to wait quietly before God. Psalm 37:34 says, "Wait on the LORD, and keep His way...."

When we wait quietly before God, the Holy Spirit will show us God's way for our life.

4. Declare God's Will

Once we know God's will, we can begin to declare it for our lives through a biblical, positive confession of the grace of God to accomplish it in our lives.

Jesus declared the Father's will and made a positive confession with these words: "This is the will of the Father who sent Me, that of all He has given Me I should lose nothing, but should raise it up at the last day" (John 6:39).

This positive confession does not in itself cause God's will to be done. Neither is it a vain religious exercise in mind over matter where we try to force God's will by repeating religious phrases. It is our way of agreeing with God, declaring His will with authority to every demonic spirit that would try to keep us from implementing it in our own lives.

As we declare God's will, God Himself will work through us to accomplish His will through the creative power of His word. Paul reminds us with these words: "For it is God who works in you both to will and to do for His good pleasure" (Phil. 2:13).

5. Obey God's Will

The last step is to obey God's will. Jesus said, "And He who sent Me is with Me. The Father has not left Me alone, for I always do those things that please Him" (John 8:29).

Once we know the will of God, we do it. We order our lives and commit all of our resources to see that it gets done. This requires a life style of supernatural praying and fasting, coupled with obedience.

Jesus said that God the Father was with Him helping Him to do those things that pleased Him. Likewise, Jesus promised to always be with us as we too seek to do God's will (Matt. 28:20).

If you have difficulty discovering God's will, it would be helpful for you to get alone with God for a time of prayer and fasting. That is how Daniel learned the will of God for the Jewish people when they were in captivity in Babylon. Daniel said, "Then I set my face toward the Lord God to make request by prayer and supplications, with fasting, sackcloth, and ashes" (Dan. 9:3).

God answered Daniel's prayer, and He will answer yours when you seek Him through supernatural prayer and fasting.

Personal Prayer

Heavenly Father, I want You to be glorified in my life. I ask You to purify my motives and cleanse me of sin so I may walk blameless before You. I choose to forgive those who have hurt me, as You have forgiven me of even greater hurts.

I desire to be in right relationship with my family, friends and acquaintances so there is no conflict in my personal relationships with others.

Lord, I want to know Your will for my life. I ask You to reveal it to me and help me to believe and receive all You have for me.

Thank You, Jesus, for Your victory over satan. I confess that You are Lord over the spirit world and that all demonic spirits must bow to Your will for my life.

Holy Spirit, I thank You for renewing my mind with the mind of Christ, giving peace to my emotions, and empowering my will to do the will of the Father. Amen.

Personal Application

1. Make a list of your unanswered prayers.

2. Write down the eight reasons that hinder prayer from being answered.

3. Ask God to show you which reason(s) may be hindering your prayers.

4. Determine what you must do to enable God to answer your prayers.

5

Praying With Persistence

In Chapter 3, we briefly discussed the importance of being persistent in our prayers. In my early walk with God, I was very puzzled about this aspect of prayer. Why would God, who is perfectly able to answer my prayers, want me to be persistent? This was somewhat of a mystery to me.

Have you ever wondered about this? It's almost like God is teasing us. He promises to answer our prayers but then requires us to coerce Him to do so. At least, it seemed that way to me. Some people even believe that if you pray more than once for the same thing, it shows a lack of faith. This can all be very confusing. Are we supposed to beg a reluctant God to help us, or do we pray one time only and forget about it?

Proper answers to these hard questions are vital for supernatural prayer and fasting. In this chapter, we'll see what the Bible says about it and why it is necessary.

Jesus gave a very important teaching about persistence in prayer. He said, "So I say to you, ask, and it will be given to you; seek, and you will find; knock, and it will be opened to you. For everyone who asks receives, and he who seeks finds, and to him who knocks it will be opened" (Luke 11:9-10).

Jesus said we should ask, seek and knock. When these words of Jesus were written in the original Greek language of the New Testament, they were written in the present tense. That means they are continuous action words. Today we would say, "keep on" asking, "keep on" seeking and "keep on" knocking. In other words, we should be persistent.

A Midnight Caller

Jesus often taught with parables. A parable is a story someone tells for the purpose of illustrating an important truth or principle. Jesus told two interesting parables that illustrate the importance of being persistent when we pray.

The first parable is the story of a midnight caller who disturbed his neighbor, asking for bread. The story is as follows:

And He said to them, "Which of you shall have a friend, and go to him at midnight and say to him, 'Friend, lend me three loaves; for a friend of mine has come to me on his journey, and I have nothing to set before him'; and he will answer from within and say, 'Do not trouble me; the door is now shut, and my children are with me in bed; I cannot rise and give to you'? I say to you, though he will not rise and give to him because he is his friend, yet because of his persistence he will rise and give him as many as he needs." (Luke 11:5-8)

In this story, a person has taken a trip to see his friend. He arrives late at night, and he's hungry. Now in Bible times, there were no McDonald's, Kentucky Fried Chicken's, Stuckey's, or other fast food restaurants where travelers could stop for a snack. So as a way of showing hospitality, it was customary for the hosts to feed their guests when the weary, hungry travelers arrived—no matter what time it was.

When this host went to feed his guest, he discovered that his pantry was empty. This was really embarrassing. Of course, it would be a disgrace for him not to provide a late-night snack for his guest.

The host, therefore, puts on his clothes, lights his lamp, and goes to the neighbor's house to ask for some bread.

Since it's midnight, the neighbor is sound asleep—but not for long. The embarrassed host is outside his neighbor's door banging on it as loud as he can. He probably awakened not only his neighbor, but everyone else on the block as well.

Can you visualize this scene? How would you like someone knocking on your door at midnight wanting to borrow a loaf of bread? That does not make for good neighborly relations.

The sleepy neighbor is obviously irritated. Not only has he been disturbed, but his children have been awakened also. Wonder how long it took him to get the kids to sleep? We can certainly understand his response.

However, the embarrassed host wouldn't give up. He "kept on" asking, seeking and knocking. The sleepy neighbor finally realized he would never get any sleep (nor get his kids quiet) until he gave his neighbor the bread. He got out of bed, stumbled around in the dark, fumbled through the pantry, opened the door part way, shoved the bread in his neighbor's hands, slammed the door, and got back in bed.

Jesus said the sleeping neighbor got out of bed at midnight and gave his friend the bread, not because he was his friend, but because of the friend's persistence.

When I first read this story I was very confused. I thought Jesus was saying that God was asleep and we had to keep banging on the door of Heaven to awaken Him. That was not His point. The focus of the story is not the sleeping neighbor, but the persistent friend.

I was so relieved to discover that God is neither sleeping on the job nor reluctant to answer our prayers. But just as circumstances required the embarrassed host to be persistent, there are reasons for why we also need to persist. We'll learn what these reasons are shortly.

A Bothersome Widow

The next parable Jesus told to illustrate our need to be persistent is the case of the bothersome widow. Here's the story.

> ..."There was in a certain city a judge who did not fear God nor regard man. Now there was a widow in that city; and she came to him, saying, 'Get justice for me from my adversary.' And he would not for a while; but afterward he said within himself, 'Though I do not fear God nor regard man, yet because this widow troubles me I will avenge her, lest by her continual coming she weary me.' " (Luke 18:2-5)

This story paints a powerful word picture for us about the need for persistence. I can just imagine this uncaring judge arriving early in the morning at the gates of the city where cases were heard. He's a hard man who could care less about justice.

A certain widow, who has a grievance, appeals to him for help, but he won't listen to her. Yet she is persistent. She won't give up. She's probably the first to arrive at the gates every morning.

The judge continues to ignore her, but she refuses to be ignored. After a while, the judge realizes the woman is not going to leave him alone. She's not going to go away. She will stay there until he gives her justice. Finally, he vindicates her because of her persistence.

In telling this story, Jesus was not suggesting that God is like the mean judge. God is ready, willing and able to help us. We do not have to make a nuisance of ourselves before God will answer our prayers.

No, the focus of this story is not on the judge; it is on the woman. There are times when we must be persistent. God honors tenacity.

A Persistent Prophet

In addition to those parables, there are many examples in the Bible that teach us the importance of persistent praying. Let's consider three of these.

The first example is the prophet Elijah. God told Elijah to go to the city of Zarephath and stay in the house of a widow. While he was there, the widow's son got sick and died.

Elijah felt compassion for the widow and her son. So he did what any true prophet would do; he prayed for the boy to be revived.

I have the blessing of praying for a lot of people, but not like Elijah prayed for this boy. Elijah laid the boy's dead body on the bed and then laid on top of the boy, while asking God to revive him. (I don't care to get that close to dead bodies.)

Now many of us would pray one time only and stop—but not Elijah. He prayed until God answered his prayer and revived the boy. It took three times before the prayer was answered.

We read the following account: "And he stretched himself out on the child three times, and cried out to the LORD and said, 'O LORD my God, I pray, let this child's soul come back to him.' Then the LORD heard the voice of Elijah; and the soul of the child came back to him, and he revived" (1 Kings 17:21-22).

I don't know why Elijah had to pray three times before he received the answer to his prayer. The exact number of times he prayed doesn't seem important. What is important is that he kept praying until the boy was revived. He didn't give up, and neither should we.

On another occasion Elijah was praying for rain. He was on Mount Carmel, which overlooks the Mediterranean Sea. I've been there a number of times myself. It's a beautiful view of the city of Haifa and the Mediterranean coast. But Elijah wasn't looking at the view. He was looking to God in prayer. He prayed seven times before getting his answer.

First Kings reads, "...And Elijah went up to the top of Carmel; then he bowed down on the ground, and put his face between his knees, and said to his servant, 'Go up now, look toward the sea.' So he went up and looked, and said, 'There is nothing.' And seven times he said, 'Go again.' Then it came to pass the seventh time, that he said, 'There is a cloud, as small as a man's hand, rising out of the sea!'...Now it happened in the meantime that the sky became black with clouds and wind, and there was a heavy rain..." (1 Kings 18:42-45).

Once again we see Elijah being persistent. In fact, the New Testament presents Elijah as an example for us to learn from regarding this aspect of prayer.

The apostle James writes, "Elijah was a man with a nature like ours, and he prayed earnestly that it would not rain; and it did not rain on the land for three years and six months. And he prayed again, and the heaven gave rain, and the earth produced its fruit" (James 5:17-18).

James tells us that Elijah prayed "earnestly." In the previous verse he said, "The effective, fervent prayer of a righteous man avails much" (James 5:16b). These words suggest a steadfast tenacity that will not quit until the answer is received.

An Inquiring Apostle

Our next example is the apostle Paul. Paul was constantly harassed by a messenger of satan that he referred to as a "thorn in the flesh." (See 2 Cor. 12:7.)

A thorn in the flesh can be very painful. It seems like every time I trim the rosebushes in my backyard, I get a thorn in the flesh. I let out a yell and carefully pull it out as fast as I can, and I don't stop pulling until it's all out. That is a time when you really want to be persistent.

Now Paul didn't have a literal thorn, but the suffering he endured was causing him great discomfort. So being human, like all the rest of us, he asked God to remove the thorn. Paul didn't like God's answer, so he asked Him a second time. Paul was hoping for an answer different from the one God gave him. But he got the same answer. He asked a third time and again got the same response from God.

Paul can tell this story better than I. Here's what he said: "Concerning this thing I pleaded with the Lord three times that it might depart from me. And He said to me, 'My grace is sufficient for you, for My strength is made perfect in weakness'..." (2 Cor. 12:8-9).

Three times Paul asked God to remove the thorn in his flesh. He continued to ask until God made it clear that His answer was final. Although God would not remove the thorn, His grace working in Paul would enable him to continue his apostolic ministry and help him overcome his adversary.

Paul was persistent. Wouldn't you be persistent if you were constantly harassed by satan? He didn't give up until the issue was settled. Neither should we give up. We may not always like God's answer, but His grace will be sufficient for the challenges we must face.

It was this same harassed apostle who wrote the following words for our encouragement: "And we know that all things work together for good to those who love God, to those who are the called according to His purpose" (Rom. 8:28).

As we have discussed in previous chapters, God has a plan and purpose for your life. He is actively working behind the scenes of your personal circumstances to help you fulfill your destiny. Although we don't always have full knowledge and understanding of how God answers prayers, we continue to pray in faith until we have His assurance in our heart.

A Burdened Savior

One last example to consider is Jesus Himself. The setting is in the Garden of Gethsemane the night Jesus is betrayed and arrested. His soul is in great distress as He ponders what lies ahead for Him. His great anguish is not about the physical suffering, but the spiritual suffering that He must endure when He bears our sins on the cross.

Jesus prayed three times for courage and strength to face the difficult challenge that awaited Him. Matthew writes, "So He left them, went away again, and prayed the third time, saying the same words" (Matt. 26:44).

Jesus was about to fulfill His destiny. Yet, in His humanity, He needed a final reassurance and comforting from His heavenly Father. He prayed twice but was still overcome by despair. Finally, after praying a third time, He found the strength and peace He needed. He was ready to face the events leading to His death on the cross.

There are many circumstances we may face that could overwhelm us in our humanity. We may present our burden to God through prayer and still feel overcome by despair. However, if we will persist, our heavenly Father will give us the courage, strength and peace we need to face the difficult challenges awaiting us in this life.

Why Persistence Is Necessary

From what we have learned so far in this chapter, it should be very clear that persistence is an important requirement to supernatural prayer and fasting. *But why is persistence necessary?* Why doesn't God do His thing without our having to persist? The answer is simple. We must persist because of satan and the sinful nature of mankind.

You see, God allows satan a limited ability to conduct spiritual warfare against us. The one thing that makes satan tremble is supernatural prayer and fasting. Satan knows better than we do the power we have through these spiritual weapons. Therefore, he does everything he can to oppose our prayers, as we learned in the previous chapter with the story about Daniel.

In addition to satan's trying to hinder God's purposes, our own human nature gets in the way of what God wants to accomplish. God has allowed us a free will that we can use to serve God or resist God. Persistent prayer often is required to bring the human will into submission to God's will.

Spiritual Warfare

We must understand that the Christian life is a life of warfare. God has chosen to allow us to participate in the struggle of the ages between good and evil. We are in a great battle, and there is no place for Christian wimps.

A problem we have in the West is identifying our enemy. We have a materialistic, rationalistic worldview that does not recognize the true nature of our enemy.

Our enemy is spiritual, not physical. Because our enemy is spiritual, our battles are spiritual. There are spiritual forces we cannot see that are actively opposing the purposes of God. These opposing forces cause conflict in the spiritual realm that is manifested in the physical realm. The cause of the conflict is not at the physical level but in the spirit realm, where opposing forces seek to control the physical realm.

The apostle Paul says it this way: "For we do not wrestle against flesh and blood, but against principalities, against powers, against the rulers of the darkness of this age, against spiritual hosts of wickedness in the heavenly places" (Eph. 6:12).

After identifying our enemy, Paul proceeds to explain the spiritual armor God has given us as Christian soldiers (verses 13-17). He then goes on to say that after we put on our spiritual armor, we pray. He writes, "Praying always with all prayer and supplication in the

Spirit, being watchful to this end with all perseverance and supplication for all the saints" (Eph. 6:18).

The incredible truth Paul is teaching us is that the battle actually takes place in the prayer closet, or wherever you pray. We go to war by getting on our knees. That is the front line of battle. It's so tragic that many Christians are "absent without leave" (AWOL). Their prayer closets are empty. It's little wonder so many are defeated.

A modern example of the "physical-spiritual" conflict is the Middle East. The constant fighting between Israel and the Arabs is not caused by political, ethnic, geographic, social, or other differences in the physical realm. It is the result of a great unseen spiritual battle taking place in the heavenlies for control of Jerusalem and the Middle East.

The anti-Western Arab dictators and terrorist groups such as the PLO and others are not our real enemies. The real enemy is the same prince of Persia (demonic powers) that sought to destroy the Jews during the time of Daniel, as we discussed earlier. In our world today, that spirit goes by the name of "Islam." This spirit will not be defeated by American military might but by the might and power of supernatural prayer and fasting.

A clear example of this spiritual battling is given in the Bible in Exodus 17. Here's what happened.

Moses was leading the Hebrews to the land God had promised them. This is the same land they are in today. Along the way, they were attacked by the Amalekites. The Amalekites were descendents of Esau (Gen. 36:12) and were a warlike people. Esau was an ancestor of the modern Arab people. So what we have here is a war between the Arabs and the Jews.

Moses sent Joshua and a volunteer army to fight the Amalekites at the physical level. But Moses went to the top of a hill to fight the Amalekites at the spiritual level. He held the "rod of God" in his hand. This rod was the symbol of God's power working on behalf of the Hebrew people as Moses prayed for victory.

Exodus 17:9-13 reads:

And Moses said to Joshua, "Choose us some men and go out, fight with Amalek. Tomorrow I will stand on the top of the hill with the rod of God in my hand." So Joshua did as Moses said to him, and fought with Amalek. And Moses, Aaron, and Hur went up to the top of the hill. And so it was, when Moses held up his hand, that Israel prevailed; and when he let down his hand, Amalek prevailed. But Moses' hands became heavy; so they took a stone and put it under him, and he sat on it. And Aaron and Hur supported his hands, one on one side, and the other on the other side; and his hands were steady until the going down of the sun. So Joshua defeated Amalek and his people with the edge of the sword.

This story gives us tremendous insight into the true nature of our battles in life and the need for prayer.

As long as Moses raised the rod of God and prayed (the spiritual battle), Joshua defeated the Amalekites (the physical battle). But when Moses grew weary and could no longer hold up the rod of God, Joshua was defeated.

This is just as true for our lives today as it was for the children of Israel. Our enemy is not the Amalekites (human conflicts), but wicked, oppressive spirits that seek to keep us from entering into the land of promise God has for our life. We do not fight these enemies at the physical level only. We also fight them at the spiritual level by holding high the rod of God. This rod is supernatural prayer and fasting.

Many of God's people are defeated because they do not raise this spiritual weapon against the devil. However, victory is assured when we lift it high. I pray this book will help you more clearly understand the importance and the power of this rod of God. Ask Him to help you use it more effectively in defeating the spiritual Amalekites that war against you. Dear friend, they are already defeated! Take your God-given authority over them through supernatural prayer and fasting.

Preparing the Human Heart

A second reason we must persist in prayer is our own unreadiness to properly respond to the answer God has for us. This is true for ourselves as well as for those for whom we are praying. We call this period of expectation, "waiting on God." God calls it, "waiting on us." He is waiting for us to be transformed in character so He can entrust us with the answer.

Quite frankly, there are times when we are just too spiritually immature for God to grant us our request. If God always gave us what we wanted when we wanted it, our inability to properly handle His answer would cause disaster. We would certainly do more harm than good. (Smile!)

A story in the Bible provides a good example of this point. It's the story of Hannah. Hannah was married to a man named Elkanah. Perhaps because Hannah was barren, Elkanah took a second wife named Peninnah.

Peninnah was not barren. She gave birth to a number of children. In Bible times, fertility was a sign of God's blessings. A woman who was barren was viewed as cursed by God.

The Book of First Samuel tells us that Peninnah mocked Hannah. We read, "And her rival also provoked her severely, to make her miserable, because the LORD had closed her womb" (1 Sam. 1:6).

Although Elkanah loved Hannah, he naturally directed his romantic interest toward Peninnah. And if he's going to take the kids on a picnic, he might as well leave Hannah at home. The rivalry between the two women was obvious.

We can certainly understand Hannah's frustrations and disappointments. She so desperately wanted a child.

116

I'm sure she could visualize the child growing up in the family as the "favorite" of Elkanah. Then she and her child would be the center of her husband's attention. That would certainly put an end to Peninnah constantly ridiculing Hannah. But her prayer was not answered. She remained barren.

Finally, in desperation, Hannah gave up all thoughts of her rivalry with Peninnah. She made a brave decision that not only changed her life, but the life of all Israel as well. She determined that if God would give her a son, she would give up the child to God.

And she was in bitterness of soul, and prayed to the LORD and wept in anguish. Then she made a vow and said, "O LORD of hosts, if You will indeed look on the affliction of Your maidservant and remember me, and not forget Your maidservant, but will give Your maidservant a male child, then I will give him to the LORD all the days of his life...."
(1 Sam. 1:10-11)

I believe that is what God was waiting to hear Hannah say. As long as she focused on her selfish interest in having a son, as natural as that interest was, she remained barren. But when she gave that interest up to God, she conceived and bore a son named Samuel.

Samuel did not live at home. He was raised by the priest at the tabernacle of the Lord. He later became a great prophet who guided the people during a difficult time of transition in the history of the fledgling nation.

117

I'd like to share a personal story with you on how I learned this lesson of laying down selfish desires.

The early years of this ministry were very difficult and certainly tried our faith. I spent six to eight hours each day studying the Bible and writing the manuscripts for my books. I wrote each manuscript word for word, without the help of a computer or dictating machine. Peggy typed them from my handwritten copies using a standard electric typewriter.

Since this required all of my time, it was not feasible for me to do much actual teaching. Therefore, I had no exposure. This lack of visibility meant that no one really knew or understood what I was doing. Also, since praying, studying and writing were intangible activities, people were not aware of the needs of the ministry. This meant we did not have a group of people to help us on a regular monthly basis with their prayers and finances. Yet, somehow God provided.

I found it difficult to explain to people what God had called me to do. Very few understood that God calls and anoints people to teach the Bible as a separate ministry from pastoring, evangelizing or other more traditionally recognized ministries. I spent a lot of time communicating to others about the role of a teacher. Some seemed to understand, but most just couldn't grasp what I was talking about.

God was sharing many powerful, life-changing insights with me, but there were few opportunities for teaching them to others. At times I thought my heart would burst if God didn't provide an outlet for sharing the wonderful truths He was putting in me.

Many times I cried out to God in desperation. I truly did not think I could live if I could not get relief from the intense desire that was overwhelming me. The only way I knew to get relief was by ministering these profound truths to others.

I wondered why God would call me to teach the Bible, yet not provide what I thought were the proper opportunities to do so. I felt lonely, misunderstood and rejected. No one seemed to care. At times I was filled with self-pity, but I was determined not to promote myself nor try to "get a following" through my own efforts. I thought if God couldn't do it, then it wasn't going to get done.

God heard the cry of my heart and gave me a word of encouragement. The words that follow are exact quotes of what God said to me. I have written them unedited, just as God spoke them to me by His Spirit.

You have been walking the road of getting to know God. You're still hanging in there and the testings are still around.

Nobody necessarily knows about you but God. No one else needs to know about you. The Creator of Heaven and earth knows everything about you. And in His way and in His time, He'll bring you forth having refined you in the fires of His testing. You shall be gold. It is the

Word of the Lord. You are being tried in the furnace of affliction. He's making gold of you. You will come forth. And then He will reward you openly.

Hang in there in the secret place. He's purifying your motives. He's wanting to see your actions and reactions when others are coming out and being used. Oh yes, others who necessarily haven't paid the price that you are paying. They push doors. They make things work in the ways of men. They announce themselves. They just want the fleshly and the spectacular. They push doors and you see them.

That's all right. They don't know the relationship that you know right now with your God. They don't hear Him like you hear Him.

Provided your motivation is right and you don't resent them or be jealous or judge or be critical but love them and support them; I tell you, provided your motivation is pure and you love and support others in the Body of Christ, truly, truly from your heart and rejoice in anything God is doing in them and through them.

You hang in there behind the scenes and God will bring you out and blow your mind and their's with the authority that He will give you when it's His time to bring you out. To elevate you? No! To more effectively make God known to a lost and dying world.

This was certainly a word of encouragement and hope. When Peggy and I heard it, we both knew instantly that God had spoken to our hearts. It was not just a word for us (*logos*), it was a word (*rhema*) directly to us from our loving heavenly Father.

Approximately three years passed before we saw this word fulfilled. During those three years, God began to purify my motives. He dealt with my pride, ego, and jealous and competitive spirit. He took away any desire I had for personal honor and recognition and gave me a servant's heart. It was slow and painful, but necessary.

I realized even more clearly that God was more interested in my knowing Him than serving Him. In fact, until I knew Him more intimately, and became more like Him, He would not let me serve Him. I discovered that this has always been God's priority and way of dealing with His servants down through the ages.

You see, there's a definite time gap between when God calls someone to a particular task and when He sends them to perform the task. That period, which we call "waiting on God," is the time we get to know God and learn His ways. It's the time His character is formed in us. It's the time we are being emptied of self so God can effectively use us for His glory.

Perhaps you have not yet received the answer to your prayer because God is preparing your heart. He is working on your character and purifying your motives. Be encouraged. There is a work God desires to do in you. He wants you to be blameless and without offense. He wants you filled with the fruits of righteousness. Yield to Him! Submit your will to Him.

Trust Him to work all circumstances in your life for His glory and your good. Delight yourself in Him, and He will give you the desires of your heart (Ps. 37:4).

Test of Faith, Sincerity and Desire

A third reason we must persist in prayer is that God uses the time of waiting to test our faith, sincerity and desire.

In an earlier chapter we read Hebrews 11:6 as part of our discussion of the prayer of faith. It would be appropriate to read it once more. "But without faith it is impossible to please Him, for he who comes to God must believe that He is, and that He is a rewarder of those who diligently seek Him" (Heb. 11:6).

God rewards us with answered prayer when we diligently seek Him. This is an earnest zeal for God and His blessings in our life. This is more than a superficial, passing interest. It is a firm resolve that will not be denied.

The Bible gives many examples of people who sought God with great determination. One story is about a Gentile woman whose daughter was demon-possessed. The mother heard that Jesus was ministering in her community, so she went to His meetings seeking help.

Because she was a Gentile, and considered unclean by the Jews, Jesus' disciples urged Him to send her away. Jesus Himself tested her. He said, "I was not sent except to the lost sheep of the house of Israel" (Matt. 15:24b).

At this point, a less determined person would have given up. But not this woman—she came even closer to Jesus and asked Him for help. Again Jesus tested her. He said, "It is not good to take the children's bread and throw it to the little dogs" (verse 26b). The Jews called Gentiles unclean dogs.

This seemingly cool reception Jesus gave the woman would have disheartened all but the most courageous, steadfast person. This woman would not be denied. She responded with a bold humility, "Yes, Lord, yet even the little dogs eat the crumbs which fall from their masters' table" (verse 27).

Jesus answered, "O woman, great is your faith! Let it be to you as you desire" (verse 28b).

Jesus gave this woman what she wanted because she wanted it bad enough to be persistent. He tested her faith, sincerity and desire.

You know, God will test ours as well. Why should God be overly concerned about our request if we're not? His level of interest will coincide with ours. His commitment to answer our prayer will be the same as our commitment to want Him to answer it. If it's really important to us, we'll do whatever is necessary to get the answer. If it's not important to us, it won't be important to God.

If often takes time for us to discover just how important it is for God to answer our prayers. Over a period of time, we may come to realize that we were not as serious with God as we thought. But when we want the answer more than we want life itself, we will have the answer.

Personal Prayer

Heavenly Father, I worship You for Your mighty ability to answer my prayers and Your gracious desire to do so. I desire that You transform me into Your image and teach me Your ways. I acknowledge that You have a perfect time for answering my prayers, and I wait patiently for Your response.

Lord Jesus, I thank You for defeating satan and all wicked spirits that follow him. You are my spiritual armor. I appropriate Your victory over satan for my own life. By Your death and resurrection, I take authority over demonic spirits that oppose Your purposes for my life. I claim Your victory as mine and I will not be denied Your blessing in my life.

Holy Spirit, I submit my will to You and ask You to produce the character of Jesus in me. Help me to persevere and empower me to pray with faith, sincerity and strong desire.

Lord, I thank You for hearing my prayer. I await Your answer with great joy and expectation.
Amen.

Personal Application

1. Explain why it is necessary to be persistent in prayer.

2. What are some reasons you have stopped praying the prayers that have not been answered?

3. How can you tell if it is God or satan delaying the answer to your prayer?

6

Praying With Intercession

In Chapter 2, we mentioned intercession as an important element of prayer. In my own view, it is the most powerful ministry God has given us. Yet it is also the most demanding.

Like the director of a play, God is actively working behind the scenes of the drama of human history to move forward His redemptive plan and purposes for mankind. Of course, the world is not aware of His workings. But like any play that has a director, God is directing world events.

That does not mean God causes the evil in our world. Satan and human sin cause the evil in our world. But God permits the evil while using it to further His own purposes. As someone has said, "All of history is 'His–story'."

God is the director of world history, and intercessors partner with Him to move the course of world events from one scene to the next.

That is why intercession is so exciting. It allows us to have a worldwide ministry. Anyone can participate. Just think, you can have a part in shaping the history and destiny of nations.

I wrote several chapters on this important subject as well as on fasting in an earlier book entitled, *How to Prepare for the Coming Revival* (Destiny Image, Shippensburg, Pennsylvania). These are such critical subjects that I have included the information from that book in this chapter and the next. (Both chapters, pages 56-83, are reprinted with permission of Destiny Image.)

The Purpose of Intercessory Prayer

The purpose of intercessory prayer is to act as an intermediary between God and man on behalf of others so that the will of God can be accomplished on the earth (Matt. 6:10).

The prophet Isaiah ministered during the time of great sin in Israel. God desired to spare the people from judgment and held back His holy anger until intercessors could begin to pray for the people. But as time passed, no one interceded. Finally, Isaiah spoke these words to the people concerning God, "He saw that there was no man, and wondered that there was no intercessor..." (Isa. 59:16).

Apparently the Hebrews failed to understand how important this was to God. As time passed, He spoke to this problem again through the prophet Ezekiel. He said, "So I sought for a man among them who would make a wall, and stand in the gap before Me on behalf of the land, that I should not destroy it; but I found no one. Therefore I have poured out My indignation on them; I have consumed them with the fire of My wrath..." (Ezek. 22:30-31).

Abraham and Sodom

There are many great examples of intercessory prayer mentioned in the Bible. Let's begin with Abraham.

Around the year 2,000 B.C., God appeared to Abraham and told Abraham of His plans to destroy the wicked cities of Sodom and Gomorrah. This troubled Abraham greatly, so he began to intercede with God on behalf of the people. Abraham asked God, "...Would You also destroy the righteous with the wicked?" (Gen. 18:23)

Abraham then began to bargain with God. He asked God to spare the city if just 50 righteous people could be found. God agreed! Abraham must have given a big sigh of relief and somehow found the courage to bargain even harder. He asked God to spare the city if just 45 righteous could be found. Then 40, 30, 20 and 10. Each time God agreed.

Unfortunately, God could not find even ten righteous people in the towns of Sodom and Gomorrah, so He had to destroy them by fire after allowing Lot and his family to escape.

We learn from this story that one intercessor can make the difference in the destiny of an entire city. I'm sure the city council at Sodom was busy making plans for the many wicked activities they would promote in the city during the next months. But the future of the city was not in their hands. It was in the hands of one man who had access to God.

The news media often talks about the power of government and the politicians who seem to run the country. But the most powerful people on earth are not the politicians. *The most powerful people on earth are the intercessors, because they have access to God, who rules over nations.*

I have discovered through my study of the Bible and secular history, as well as from personal experience, that world powers rise and fall as the people of God rise and fall to their knees. You can make a difference in your family, your community, your state, your country and even the world events through fervent intercessory prayer.

As former President Reagan expressed it, "Let us also reflect that in the prayers of simple people there is more power and might than that possessed by all the great statesmen or armies of the earth" (Address to the Nation, December 10, 1987).

Moses at Sinai

Our next example of intercession took place around 1500 B.C. While Moses was having his mountaintop experience with God, the children of Israel were down below worshiping a golden calf. They must have had a short memory because they gave the golden calf credit for delivering them from Egypt. Needless to say, God was not pleased with this memory lapse. After letting Moses in on what was happening below, He threatened to destroy the Hebrews and start again with Moses.

Moses was greatly distressed and began to intercede on behalf of the people. We read in Exodus:

Then Moses pleaded with the LORD his God, and said: "LORD, why does Your wrath burn hot against Your people whom You have brought out of the land of Egypt with great power and with a mighty hand? Why should the Egyptians speak, and say, 'He brought them out to harm them, to kill them in the mountains, and to consume them from the face of the earth'? Turn from Your fierce wrath, and relent from this harm to Your people. Remember Abraham, Isaac, and Israel, Your servants, to whom You swore by Your own self, and said to them, 'I will multiply your descendants as the stars of the heaven; and all this land that I have spoken of I give to your descendants, and they shall inherit it forever.'" So the LORD relented from the harm which He said He would do to His people. (Ex. 32:11-14)

We all have family members and friends who, like the children of Israel, have golden calves in their lives. They are not literal golden calves, but anything that people put ahead of God. This is certainly a concern

131

to God and should be to us as well. You can postpone God's judgment on their sins, and give them further time to repent, by pleading for God's mercy through intercessory prayer.

Peter's Great Escape

One of the most powerful, yet humorous, examples of intercessory prayer is recorded in the Book of Acts. Here's what happened.

King Herod arrested Peter during the week of Passover and placed him under the guard of 16 soldiers. Herod intended to execute Peter, who was double-chained between two of the guards the night before he was to be killed.

When word reached the believers in Jerusalem about Peter's imprisonment and imminent death, they began to pray. Luke wrote, "Peter was therefore kept in prison, but constant [earnest] prayer was offered to God for him by the church" (Acts 12:5).

God heard their prayers and sent an angel to deliver Peter, who was asleep when the angel appeared. The angel gave Peter a "holy slap" to awaken him and escorted him safely past the guards and outside the prison gate.

Peter was unsure what was taking place and thought his great escape was just a dream or vision. But once he was outside the prison gate and walking the street, he realized that God had sent an angel to deliver him, and that he was now free.

When he came to his senses, he went to the house where the believers were praying and knocked at the door. Luke wrote, "So, when he had considered this, he came to the house of Mary, the mother of John whose surname was Mark, where many were gathered together praying" (Acts 12:12). A young girl named Rhoda came to answer the door, and when she realized it was Peter, she was overcome with joy and shouted the good news to everyone.

But these great prayer warriors didn't believe her. Instead of going to the door to see for themselves, they continued to ask God to deliver Peter from prison and spare his life.

Finally, at the girl's insistence, they stopped praying long enough to go to the door. When they realized it truly was Peter, they quickly let him into the house. After he told them what had happened, they sent him to a safer location. (See Acts 12:1-19.)

Peter was in a literal prison. But there are many who are in spiritual prisons. They are bound up with chains of oppression, depression, fear, poverty, disease, sin and rebellion. Satan desires to take their lives, and he has assigned his demon soldiers to guard them. Your earnest intercession can set them free as did the prayers of the believers on behalf of Peter.

The Perfect Intercessor

There are many other examples in the Bible, and history, of ordinary men and women whose intercession changed the course of world events. But the greatest intercessor of all times is Jesus Christ.

The writer of Hebrews tells us why Jesus is the perfect intercessor we all need. He wrote, "But He [Jesus], because He continues forever, has an unchangeable priesthood. Therefore He is also able to save to the uttermost [completely or forever] those who come to God through Him, since He always lives to make intercession for them" (Heb. 7:24-25).

In the ancient world, people turned away from God and no longer knew Him. But God is merciful and desired to make Himself known. The way He did this was to choose the descendents of Abraham as the ethnic people through which He would reveal Himself to the nations.

God selected a particular family to be the priests who would intercede for the nation of Israel. Aaron was the first High Priest. At his death, he was succeeded by his oldest son. This way the priesthood would be passed down from generation to generation. (See Ex. 28–29 and Lev. 8.)

But Aaron and his sons were imperfect just like all the rest of us. They had imperfect animal sacrifices to offer to God. Therefore, the job of the High Priest was never finished. He had to keep offering the same sacrifices year after year, for his own sins and the sins of the people. As soon as he got good at being a priest, he would die. Yet God, in His grace, accepted the High Priest as the intercessor for the people until one greater than Aaron would come along.

This "Greater One" is the Lord Jesus Christ! He was God in human flesh, who laid aside His own glory to be our once-and-for-all sacrifice. He humbled Himself and died on the cross, taking the consequences of our sins in His spirit, our sorrows in His soul, and our sickness and diseases in His flesh. (See Phil. 2:9-11.)

Isaiah explained it this way: "Surely He has borne our griefs and carried our sorrows; yet we esteemed Him stricken, smitten by God, and afflicted. But He was wounded for our transgressions, He was bruised for our iniquities; the chastisement for our peace was upon Him, and by His stripes we are healed" (Isa. 53:4-5).

Jesus became the ultimate intercessor when He who knew no sin became sin for us on the cross (2 Cor. 5:21). But death and the grave could not hold Him. He was raised on the third day and returned to Heaven, to minister at the right hand of God on our behalf.

We have been forgiven and made whole, once and for all, by the blood of Jesus Christ. He is the perfect sacrifice. His shed blood accomplished what the blood of animals could never do. His blood didn't just cover our sins; it took them away to be remembered no more. Therefore Jesus doesn't offer Himself again and again like the High Priest who continually offered the animals.

Unlike the High Priest of ancient times, Jesus lives forever. Therefore, He is always there to take our concerns to God and intercede on our behalf. He is exactly the kind of High Priest we need.

In view of this, Paul wrote, "Be anxious for nothing, but in everything by prayer and supplication, with thanksgiving, let your requests be made known to God; and the peace of God, which surpasses all understanding, will guard your hearts and minds through Christ Jesus" (Phil. 4:6-7).

Peter wrote the following words of encouragement, "Cast all your anxieties [cares] on Him, for He cares about you" (1 Pet. 5:7 RSV).

Principles of Intercession

It's wonderful to know that God cares for us and has provided the ministry of intercession for us and to us through Jesus Christ. It's exciting to realize that we can have such a profound influence on people and events through fervent prayer. But how do we actually pray a powerful prayer of intercession?

There are seven basic principles to guide us in making our intercession effective. Let's now consider each of them for the purpose of learning how to apply them to our lives.

1. Burdened by God to Pray

The first principle is that the intercessor is burdened by God to pray. In about the year 425 B.C., God spoke to a man named Malachi and stirred his heart for the people of Israel that they might return to God.

Here's the way the Bible expresses it: "The burden of the word of the LORD to Israel by Malachi" (Mal. 1:1).

Malachi spoke of the "burden of the Word of the Lord." What did he mean by this? The burden of the Word of the Lord is an overwhelming concern for God's glory, God's plans, God's purposes and God's people to be established on the earth. It is more than just a casual concern or passing interest.

This is a God-initiated fire that burns in your heart. It is a holy zeal for the things of God to be manifested in a specific area of concern to God which He has put in your heart.

The Bible says if you will draw near to God, He will draw near to you and reveal to you those things that concern Him on the earth. (See James 4:8 and Ps. 25:14.)

God takes a particular burden or concern that is on His heart and transfers it to your heart. It's now in His heart and yours. His burden becomes your burden. His concern becomes your concern. You become God's prayer partner, interceding with Jesus Christ for God's will to be manifested in a special or specific way on the earth. The burden will not be lifted, and you will not stop interceding, until you see the prayer answered.

2. Clean on the Inside

In order for us to be effective as intercessors, we must have clean hearts and no unconfessed sin.

When King David sinned, his fellowship with God was broken. This caused him much sadness and grief. His greatest desire was to be restored to God.

David cried out to God, "Have mercy upon me, O God, according to Your lovingkindness; according to the multitude of Your tender mercies, blot out my transgressions. Wash me thoroughly from my iniquity, and cleanse me from my sin...Create in me a clean heart, O God, and renew a steadfast [right] spirit within me. Do not cast me away from Your presence, and do not take Your Holy Spirit from me" (Ps. 51:1-2; 10-11).

Although David was just a man and made many mistakes, he desired God's presence above everything else in his life. In fact, the Bible gives the highest commendation to David. It says he was a man after God's own heart (Acts 13:22).

As intercessors, we must have such hearts for God that we will desire to be morally pure and without blame. We must be so concerned for the glory of God and His redemptive purposes that we will make sure there is nothing within us that would hinder the burden of the Word of the Lord from being accomplished. And if we discover something in our lives that is not pleasing to God, we will quickly turn from it.

James gives a hard word that many will not receive; but intercessors will, because they know how necessary it is for their walk with God. James wrote, "Draw near to God and He will draw near to you. Cleanse your hands, you sinners; and purify your hearts, you double-minded. Lament and mourn and weep! Let your laughter be turned to mourning and your joy to gloom. Humble yourselves in the sight of the Lord, and He will lift you up" (James 4:8-10).

3. Not Concerned With Personal Needs

One stumbling block to many people that keeps them from God is their desire for personal comfort, security and possessions. They will serve God if it's convenient and not too costly.

But the intercessor is different. Intercessors are not concerned about personal comforts. They will make any sacrifice necessary in order to see the burden of the Word of God fulfilled.

The prophet Ezekiel is an extreme example of this. Because of Israel's sin, God allowed the Babylonian armies to invade and conquer the land. As a way of warning the people, God called Ezekiel to prophesy about the coming destruction of Jerusalem.

Not only did Ezekiel prophesy about the coming invasion, he also had to act out his words so the people could have a visual aid of what was going to happen. (See Ezek. 4-5.)

God required Ezekiel to lie on his left side, one day for each year that the northern kingdom of Israel would be in captivity. Then God required Ezekiel to lie on his right side, one day for each year that the southern kingdom of Israel would be in captivity.

During this time, Ezekiel was limited to one meal a day. This "meal" consisted of eight ounces of defiled bread and one quart of water. The purpose of Ezekiel's plight was to dramatically illustrate to the people the rationing of bread and water which would occur during the siege of Jerusalem, because only small amounts would be available.

Furthermore, God instructed Ezekiel to shave his head and beard, and weigh it into three equal parts. He was to burn a third, slash another third with his knife, and scatter the last third to the wind. This was God's way of showing the people their fate: one-third would die from famine and disease, one-third would be killed by the enemy, and one-third would be scattered.

This was certainly not a pleasant experience for Ezekiel. But he was willing to do whatever was required to warn the people, with the hope that they would turn from their sins.

We learn from this example that the true intercessor is willing to pay any price to see the burden of the Word of God manifested. It is the intercessor's primary reason for living and the focus of his life. It sets the course and direction of his life. He becomes single-minded and will do whatever is required to bring it to fulfillment. Personal needs and creature comforts are not even a consideration for one whose heart has been burdened with the Word of the Lord.

Jesus expressed this attitude when He said, "My food is to do the will of Him who sent Me, and to finish His work" (John 4:34).

4. Conducts Spiritual Warfare

The intercessor is like the front-line foot soldier in the war against satan. Intercessors conduct spiritual warfare on behalf of others.

The Pharisees were jealous of Jesus and confused as to who He was and what He was doing. On one occasion when Jesus cast demons out of a man, the Pharisees accused Him of getting His power from satan.

Jesus showed the foolishness of this accusation and then spoke about the necessity of binding satan, who He referred to as the strong man. Matthew recorded these words from Jesus, "Or how can one enter a strong man's house and plunder his goods, unless he first binds the strong man? And then he will plunder his house" (Matt. 12:29).

It seems that satan has assigned ruling spirits to carry out his commands over the nations for the purpose of bringing humanity under his authority and control. (See Eph. 6:10-12.) These ruling spirits seek to establish strongholds over all structures of society, including the government (national and local), the media, educational organizations, recreational and leisure activities, religious organizations (including local churches) and even families, which he attacks through familiar spirits.

Intercessors conduct spiritual warfare by identifying and binding these powers of darkness and by loosing the power of God.

Jesus spoke of this ministry of the intercessor with these words, "And I will give you the keys of the kingdom of heaven, and whatever you bind on earth will be bound in heaven, and whatever you loose on earth will be loosed in heaven" (Matt. 16:19).

A casual reading of this text seems to indicate that the binding and loosing will take place in the future. To our way of thinking, the phrases "will give" and "will be" speak of something that will happen in the future.

But when this Scripture was written in the original language, the phrases were in the past tense. We would write it today as, "I have given you the keys of the kingdom of heaven, and whatever you bind on earth has already been bound in heaven, and whatever your loose on earth has already been loosed in heaven."

This means that from eternity past, God has purposed within Himself to establish His plan of redemption on the earth and has made available every provision to us so that we might pray it into being. We simply decree His will to be done and, through our intercession, both bind the forces of evil that would hinder it and loose God's redemptive power and grace.

Paul stated it this way: "For though we walk in the flesh, we do not war according to the flesh. For the weapons of our warfare are not carnal but mighty in God for pulling down strongholds, casting down arguments and every high thing that exalts itself against the knowledge of God, bringing every thought into captivity to the obedience of Christ" (2 Cor. 10:3-5).

5. Identifies With Others

One challenging aspect of intercession is the need to identify with those for whom we are interceding. This is necessary in order for us to fully relate to the needs of the people and the circumstances for which we are praying.

The Bible teaches that because He became one of us, God is able to relate to all the needs and hurts of humanity. The writer of Hebrews said, "Inasmuch then as the children have partaken of flesh and blood, He Himself likewise shared in the same, that through death He might destroy him who had the power of death, that is, the devil" (Heb. 2:14).

You know, it is very easy to give money to a visiting missionary who may be preaching in a Sunday service at our church. No effort is required to put a few dollars in the collection plate as it is being passed. But it requires a real sacrifice to spend our vacation with the missionary, eating what he eats, sleeping where he sleeps, living in the conditions where he lives, and sharing his problems and circumstances.

After sharing his life, we are better able to identify with the missionary's needs and fully relate to his situation.

And I'm sure we would be much more generous with our offering the next time the collection plate was passed for him.

6. Listens and Declares

Another important principle of intercession is that the one interceding listens to God's voice and speaks or declares what God says. This means we must listen to God's voice during the time of intercession. Instead of doing all the talking ourselves, we should have a time of silent waiting for God to speak.

Jesus said, "My sheep hear My voice..." (John 10:27). The best time to hear His voice is during times of intercession.

We learned previously from the writer of Hebrews that Jesus is at the right hand of God making intercession for us (Heb. 7:24-25). He is our intercessor in Heaven, who knows the mind of God and His perfect will. He is able to communicate this to us through the Holy Spirit, who is our intercessor on earth.

The Holy Spirit lives in all believers. He is the link between Heaven and earth. He alone on the earth knows the prayer of Jesus in Heaven, and He speaks it to our hearts and minds when we listen for His voice.

Here's how Paul stated it:

..."*Eye has not seen, nor ear heard, nor have entered into the heart of man the things which God has prepared for those who love Him."* But God has revealed*

144

them to us through His Spirit. For the Spirit searches all things, yes, the deep things of God. For what man knows the things of a man except the spirit of the man which is in him? Even so no one knows the things of God except the Spirit of God. Now we have received, not the spirit of the world, but the Spirit who is from God, that we might know the things that have been freely given to us by God. (1 Cor. 2:9-12)

The Holy Spirit intercedes for us and through us, helping us to know the mind of Christ so that His prayer in Heaven becomes our prayer on earth. We then speak or declare this revealed will of God so that it might be manifested on the earth.

Paul further explained with these words, "Likewise the Spirit also helps in our weaknesses. For we do not know what we should pray for as we ought, but the Spirit Himself makes intercession for us with groanings which cannot be uttered. Now He who searches the hearts knows what the mind of the Spirit is, because He makes intercession for the saints according to the will of God" (Rom. 8:26-27).

7. Meets the Need

Finally, the intercessor meets the prayer need whenever it is possible and wise to do so.

God created us in His image and after His likeness so that we could know Him and have fellowship with Him. When Adam and Eve sinned, man's fellowship with God was broken. This grieved God. But because

He loves us, God did something about the situation. He sent His Son to die for our sins so that we might be reconciled to Him.

The Bible says, "For God so loved the world that He gave His only begotten Son, that whoever believes in Him should not perish but have everlasting life" (John 3:16).

If we can do something to help a person or change a situation, action is required, not prayer! If we can be the answer to our own prayer, we don't need to pray; we need to act with love and wisdom.

For example, if a hard-working Christian friend loses his or her job and can't pay the bills, we don't need to grab the person's hand and ask God to help the person. Instead, we should grab our checkbooks and pay the person's bills.

The Bible puts it this way: "By this we know love, because He laid down His life for us. And we also ought to lay down our lives for the brethren. But whoever has this world's goods, and sees his brother in need, and shuts up his heart from him, how does the love of God abide in him? My little children, let us not love in word or in tongue, but in deed and in truth" (1 John 3:16-18).

I hope that through this discussion you can see the necessity of intercessory prayer and the importance of your role as a prayer partner with God. I encourage you to commit yourself to this vital, dynamic ministry so that you can help change the world. Ask God to show you what He thinks is important. Ask Him to ignite your heart with a fire that cannot be quenched.... Ask Him to give you a holy zeal for His glory, His plans, His purposes and His people. And may God bless you as you labor to bring the burden of the Word of the Lord from Heaven to earth.

Personal Prayer

*Heavenly Father, I praise You for Your great plan
of redemption for mankind. I acknowledge that You
are the Sovereign God of history. You are the Governor
among the nations. The flow of history is simply the un-
folding of Your plan to achieve Your eternal purpose.
I declare that Your counsel shall stand and You will
accomplish all that You purpose.*

*Jesus, I acknowledge that You are King of kings and
Lord of lords. The kingdoms of this world belong to You.
The government of this world shall be upon Your shoul-
ders and of the increase of Your government
there shall be no end.*

*Holy Spirit, I thank You that You are actively working
to move forward the flow of history. You are directing
world events for the glory of God, the good of God's
people, and the destruction of the wicked.*

*Lord, I want to be a part of what You are doing in
the world today. I want to participate with You as an
intercessor to shape the course of history and the
destiny of nations.*

*In accordance with Your wisdom and power, I forbid
every spiritual enemy that opposes You to further deceive
and destroy or hinder Your purposes from being fulfilled.
I stand firm against them and declare their defeat.*

*I ask You now, Lord, to send a mighty revival to
Your Church, convict unbelievers, orchestrate
international affairs according to Your good*

pleasure, make a way for the gospel of the Kingdom to be preached to all nations and fulfill Your covenant promises to Your ancient people, Israel.

Lord, I praise You for all that You are doing, and I thank You for allowing me to be part of it. I commit myself to be a watchman who will stand in the gap until Your purposes are fully manifested on the earth. Amen.

Personal Application

1. What is the primary purpose of intercessory prayer?

2. State four examples of intercession recorded in the Bible.

3. List the seven principles of intercession and determine how each can apply to your life.

4. Ask God to give you a burden for the things that concern Him about your family, church, community, national and international affairs, etc. Seek God's purposes for the burden He gives you. Identify strongholds that are hindering God's work and oppose them through your intercession.

7

Praying With Fasting

Fellowship with God includes one of the most important disciplines practiced by Christians down through the ages. Yet, it is one of the most neglected in our modern times. This is the biblically-sanctioned practice of fasting.

Peggy and I have practiced fasting for many years as a regular discipline in our walk with God. We have always found it to be a blessing to our personal lives as well as a powerful means for battling demonic forces. It is a vital aid to supernatural prayer and a major key to triumphant living.

Fasting is certainly not a normal part of life in our Western, pleasure-seeking, self-gratifying society. When it is brought to our attention, we generally think of it as an antiquated custom, which is sometimes practiced by people we tend to view as a bit radical in their thinking.

Yet, you may be surprised to know that fasting was a required part of Jewish religious life, as well as a common practice in the lives of Jesus, first-century believers, and both Christians and non-Christians throughout history.

Fasting has always had a significant role as a spiritual discipline that precedes revival, and the revelation and manifestation of the glory of God. For this reason, it is important for us to gain an understanding of fasting and how we can practice it as an act of faith....

What Is Fasting?

The most basic definition of biblical fasting is to abstain from food and/or drink for religious purposes. Biblical fasting relates to spiritual matters and is usually practiced when our concern for God's interests requires a more intense level of commitment and preparation than normal. Fasting is usually practiced temporarily for a pre-determined length of time, although many people do fast on a regular basis.

The Purpose of Fasting

The purpose of fasting is to concentrate our attention on moral and spiritual concerns as a higher priority in our life than fleshly appetites. It necessarily involves self-denial.

Of course, self does not like to be denied. But when we are burdened with the Word of the Lord, our concern and zeal for the things of God becomes a stronger motivation to us than our desire for food.

The prophet Isaiah wrote the classic chapter in the Bible on fasting. (See Isaiah 58.) I suggest that you take the time to read this entire chapter. In the key verse of the chapter, God spoke through Isaiah and said, "Is this not the fast that I have chosen: to loose the bonds of wickedness, to undo the heavy burdens, to let the oppressed go free, and that you break every yoke?" (Isa. 58:6) Here we discover the true purpose of fasting.

We learn from the pen of Isaiah that fasting is a means to an end. The end is to bring moral and spiritual renewal with the result being that God is glorified and people are set free from sin and demonic oppression. Perhaps this is why satan has blinded our eyes to the importance of fasting as a spiritual weapon.

Fasting in the Old Testament

The Bible has much to say about fasting. The word *fast* in its various forms is mentioned approximately 78 times. In addition, the biblical phrase "afflict your souls" involved a humbling of the people before God that always included fasting.

God established the Jewish Day of Atonement as a national day of "soul affliction" which included fasting. (See Lev. 16:29-31 and 23:27-32.)

Moses fasted 40 days and nights when he received the commandments from God. He continued this another 40 days and nights while he interceded for the people after they sinned by making the golden calf idol. (See Ex. 34:28 and Deut. 9:18.)

King David fasted for the life of his firstborn. We read in the Second Book of Samuel, "David therefore pleaded with God for the child, and David fasted and went in and lay all night on the ground" (2 Sam. 12:16).

David must have fasted frequently. He wrote these words, "...I humbled myself with fasting..." (Ps. 35:13). In Psalm 69:10 he said, "When I wept and chastened my soul with fasting...." And another time he wrote, "My knees are weak through fasting, and my flesh is feeble from lack of fatness" (Ps. 109:24).

Ezra fasted for protection when leading a group of exiles back from Babylon to Jerusalem. He wrote, "Then I proclaimed a fast there at the river of Ahava, that we might humble ourselves before our God, to seek from Him the right way for us and our little ones and all our possessions...So we fasted and entreated our God for this, and He answered our prayer" (Ezra 8:21,23).

When Nehemiah heard the sad news of the state of affairs in Jerusalem, he was overcome with grief and fasted to God for help. He wrote, "So it was, when I heard these words, that I sat down and wept, and mourned for many days; I was fasting and praying before the God of heaven" (Neh. 1:4).

During one of the greatest crises in the history of Israel, God raised up Esther to intercede for her people.

The key to her success was prayer and fasting. When the king decreed that all Jews were to be killed, they fasted for deliverance. We learn from the Book of Esther: "And in every province where the king's command and decree arrived, there was great mourning among the Jews, with fasting, weeping, and wailing; and many lay in sackcloth and ashes" (Esther 4:3).

Esther decided to enter the king's court without permission, seeking to help her people. She instructed her aides, "Go, gather all the Jews who are present in Shushan, and fast for me; neither eat nor drink for three days, night or day. My maids and I will fast likewise..." (Esther 4:16).

The prophet Daniel fasted when seeking to understand the Word of God concerning the captivity of the Jews in Babylon. We read in Daniel: "Then I set my face toward the Lord God to make request by prayer and supplications, with fasting, sackcloth, and ashes" (Dan. 9:3).

Three times the prophet Joel called for fasting as a means of seeking God. Joel wrote, "Consecrate a fast, call a sacred assembly; gather the elders and all the inhabitants of the land into the house of the LORD your God, and cry out to the LORD" (Joel 1:14).

In the following chapter he wrote these words on behalf of God, " 'Now, therefore,' says the LORD, 'Turn to Me with all your heart, with fasting, with weeping, and with mourning.'...Blow the trumpet in Zion, consecrate a fast, call a sacred assembly" (Joel 2:12,15).

When Jonah preached at Nineveh, the people repented and fasted: "So the people of Nineveh believed God, proclaimed a fast, and put on sackcloth, from the greatest to the least of them" (Jon. 3:5).

Fasting in the New Testament

In the New Testament, we learn that Jesus fasted on one occasion for 40 days and nights. Matthew wrote, "And when He had fasted forty days and forty nights, afterward He was hungry" (Matt. 4:2).

John the Baptist and his followers also practiced fasting. We learn this from Matthew 9:14 when one of John's disciples came to Jesus with the following question: "Why do we and the Pharisees fast often, but Your disciples do not fast?" Although Jesus' disciples did not fast while they were with Him, they did fast after He returned to Heaven.

Believers in the early church also practiced fasting. It was during such a time that God spoke to them about the establishing of local churches. Luke wrote, "As they ministered to the Lord and fasted, the Holy Spirit said, 'Now separate to Me Barnabas and Saul for the work to which I have called them' " (Acts 13:2).

Paul certainly learned from this experience and fasted regularly. When it came time for him to appoint elders to the churches he established, he sought God through prayer and fasting. Luke said, "So when they had appointed elders in every church, and prayed with fasting, they commended them to the Lord in whom they had believed" (Acts 14:23). (See also 2 Cor. 6:5 and 11:27.)

Cornelius was a devout Gentile seeking to know God. He also sought God through prayer and fasting. We read his words in Acts: "So Cornelius said, 'Four days ago I was fasting until this hour; and at the ninth hour I prayed in my house, and behold, a man stood before me in bright clothing, and said, "Cornelius, your prayer has been heard, and your alms are remembered in the sight of God" ' " (Acts 10:30-31).

Fasting as a Way of Life

For the Christian, fasting is not a legalistic endeavor; it is expected as a way of life. Jesus said, "Moreover, when you fast, do not be like the hypocrites, with a sad countenance. For they disfigure their faces that they may appear to men to be fasting..." (Matt. 6:16).

Notice that Jesus did not say, "if" you fast. He said "when" you fast! He took it for granted that believers would fast.

When we study the history of Christianity, we discover that serious-minded believers down through the ages have practiced fasting as a means of humbling themselves before God. This includes every man and woman who has made a significant and lasting impact on the Church of Jesus Christ. Shouldn't we also make this important practice a regular part of our lives?

Degrees of Fasting

The Bible seems to indicate three degrees or levels of fasting. There are the normal fast, the limited fast and the extreme fast.

In the normal fast, the person does not eat, but he does drink the necessary liquids. This was apparently the degree of fasting Jesus practiced during His 40-day fast. Matthew pointed out that Jesus was hungry, not thirsty (Matt. 4:2).

God has made our bodies in such a way that the average person can go about 40 days without food. (Sometimes I have a problem with 40 minutes.) During this time of fasting, the body gets its nourishment from the surplus fat stored in the body. After 40 days, the body begins to consume its living cells, and the person will die if the fast is not broken.

I find it interesting that satan waited until Jesus had fasted the full 40 days before he came to tempt Jesus with the bread. This was clearly a real temptation for Jesus, which He was able to overcome through the power of God's Word.

The second degree of fasting recorded in the Bible is the limited fast. In this level of fasting, the person eats some food, but it is limited to a certain type of food. Daniel is an example of a person who practiced this level of fasting.

When Daniel was in Babylon, he and three of his friends were selected for special training to serve the king. They were told to eat certain rich foods as part of their training. These food items had most likely been offered to the Babylonian gods, which meant that Daniel and his friends could not eat them. Daniel made the following request of the steward: "Please test your servants for ten days, and let them give us vegetables to eat and water to drink" (Dan. 1:12).

Can you imagine someone wanting broccoli rather than prime rib?

But at the end of the ten-day period, Daniel and his three companions were in better physical shape than the others who had eaten the "king's dainties."

At another time, Daniel had a vision that troubled him so greatly that he prayed and fasted. We read the following account: "In those days I, Daniel, was mourning three full weeks. I ate no pleasant food, no meat or wine came into my mouth, nor did I anoint myself at all, till three whole weeks were fulfilled" (Dan. 10:2-3).

A more severe level of fasting recorded in the Bible is the extreme fast. In this level of fast, the person neither eats nor drinks.

Moses was on an extreme fast when he received the commandments from God. We read in Exodus: "So

159

he was there with the LORD forty days and forty nights; he neither ate bread nor drank water. And He wrote on the tablets the words of the covenant, the Ten Commandments" (Ex. 34:28). (See also Deut. 9:9.)

Moses repeated this extreme fast when the Hebrews sinned against God by making the golden calf. Moses said, "And I fell down before the LORD, as at the first, forty days and forty nights; I neither ate bread nor drank water, because of all your sin which you committed in doing wickedly in the sight of the LORD, to provoke Him to anger" (Deut. 9:18).

Ezra was grieved because of the sins of the people and fasted in this way. We read, "Then Ezra rose up from before the house of God, and went into the chamber of Jehohanan the son of Eliashib; and when he came there, he ate no bread and drank no water, for he mourned because of the guilt of those from the captivity" (Ezra 10:6).

In a reference we've already noted, Esther called for an extreme fast when she went in before the king (Esther 4:16).

Types of Fast

A fast may be private or public. An individual fast is a private matter between the person and God. In the Scriptures in Matthew 6:16, Jesus rebuked the religious leaders because they fasted in such a way as to impress the common people. Jesus called them hypocrites.

In ancient times, a hypocrite was an actor who wore a mask to give the appearance that he was someone other than himself. When Jesus called the Pharisees hypocrites, He was accusing them of pretending to be pious when in reality they were only seeking the praise of men.

Individual fasting must be done unto God, not men. (See Zech. 7:5.) Jesus went on to say, "But you, when you fast, anoint your head and wash your face, so that you do not appear to men to be fasting, but to your Father who is in the secret place; and your Father who sees in secret will reward you openly" (Matt. 6:17-18).

There are times as well when fasting is done collectively and publicly. The Day of Atonement mentioned earlier is an example.

There are also other examples of public fasting mentioned in the Bible. On one occasion, a civil war took place between the armies of the tribe of Benjamin and the other tribes of Israel. The armies of Benjamin won the first two battles. This prompted the entire Israeli army to weep and fast before the Lord. The Book of Judges tells us, "Then all the children of Israel, that is, all the people, went up and came to the house of God and wept. They sat there before the LORD and fasted that day until evening..." (Judg. 20:26).

Jeremiah instructed his associates to read God's Word on the public fast day (Jer. 36:6). In Scriptures mentioned previously, Joel called the nation to fast because of their sins (Joel 1:14; 2:15). The fast during the time of

Esther was also a public fast (Esther 4:16). The entire city of Nineveh fasted as a sign of repentance before God (Jon. 3:5).

The United States had its own civil war crisis that threatened to destroy the nation. President Abraham Lincoln, sensing the critical need for God's help, proclaimed a national day of fasting with these words:

> *We have been the recipients of the choicest bounties of heaven. We have been preserved, these many years, in peace and prosperity. We have grown in numbers, wealth and power, as no other nation has ever grown. But we have forgotten God. We have forgotten the gracious hand which preserved us in peace, and multiplied and enriched and strengthened us; and we have vainly imagined, in the deceitfulness of our hearts, that all these blessings were produced by some superior wisdom and virtue of our own. Intoxicated with unbroken success, we have become too self-sufficient to feel the necessity of redeeming and preserving grace, too proud to pray to the God who made us! It behooves us, then to humble ourselves before the offended power, to confess our national sins, and to pray for clemency and forgiveness.*
> (From *The Rebirth of America.* The Arthur S. DeMoss Foundation, page 151.)   Thurs, 30th April 1863

Getting Started

President Lincoln's words certainly apply to our nation today. Yet, as bleak as things appear to be, it's not too late for America to return to God.

But we must do our part! Desperate times call for desperate measures. If fasting has not been part of your life, please make it a regular practice along with fervent praying for revival to come to America through the Church in America.

As a start, it would be helpful to establish a specific time of fasting on a regular basis, such as a certain meal on a particular day or a specific day of the week.

Begin your fast on a small scale and then extend it for longer periods as your body becomes accustomed to going without food.

If you have a physical problem or take medicine, such as insulin, you should consult with your physician before attempting to fast.

There should be a specific burden for which you are fasting, although a regular fast can be for matters of a general nature that concern you. God may lead you to establish a public fast time within your local church or community as Joel indicated.

As you fast in faith, God will surely hear the cry of your heart to loose the bonds of wickedness, to undo the heavy burdens, to let the oppressed go free, and to break every yoke in your life and the lives of those around you.

Remember, it only takes one person to make a difference!

Personal Prayer

*Heavenly Father, I thank You for establishing fasting
as a means for me to draw nearer to You. I thank You
for the examples of those in the Bible and others down
through the ages who practiced fasting.*

*Lord Jesus, I thank You for Your example of fasting,
particularly when You fasted for 40 days and nights during Your time of temptation. Thank You for not
submitting to the desires of the flesh, but for resisting temptation and overcoming satan.*

*Holy Spirit, I ask You to help me follow Jesus' example
in fasting. Help me to make fasting a regular
part of my life. Help me to focus my attention more on
moral and spiritual concerns as a higher priority
in my life than on fleshly appetites. Thank You for
assisting me and hearing the cry of my heart.*
Amen.

Personal Application

1. What is the biblical meaning of fasting?

2. What is the purpose of fasting?

3. State the three degrees of fasting.

4. List the two types of fast.

5. Establish a plan to fast as a regular part of your Christian life. Consider the possibility of organizing a public fast within your local church and community.

BIBLE STUDY MATERIALS BY RICHARD BOOKER

MINISTRY IN THE LOCAL CHURCH

Richard currently spends most of his time in a traveling ministry to the local church. If you are interested in having him come to your church, contact him directly at his Houston address.

CHRISTIAN GROWTH SEMINARS

Richard conducts a series of unique seminars in the local church. Each seminar is six hours long with a workbook in which the participant writes during the seminar. Current seminars are on prayer, personal Bible study, successful Christian living, and discipleship. Brochures are available from the ministry.

LOCAL CHURCH CENTERED BIBLE SCHOOLS

Richard has developed a Christian Growth Institute, which is a nine-month Bible school designed to be taught in the local church by the pastor or his associates. A catalog is available from the ministry.

BOOKS

Richard's books are superior quality teaching books. They uniquely communicate profound life-changing Bible truths with a rich depth, freshness and simplicity, and also explain how to apply what you have read to your life. His books are described on the following pages. You may order them through your bookstore or clip and mail the Book Order Form provided in the back of this book.

THE MIRACLE OF THE SCARLET THREAD

This book explains how the Old and New Testaments are woven together by the scarlet thread of the blood covenant to tell one complete story through the Bible.

COME AND DINE

This book takes the mystery and confusion out of the Bible. It provides background information on how we got the Bible, a survey of every book in the Bible and how each relates to Jesus Christ, practical principles, forms and guidelines for your own personal Bible study, and a systematic plan for effectively reading, studying and understanding the Bible for yourself.

WHAT EVERYONE NEEDS TO KNOW ABOUT GOD

This book is about the God of the Bible. It shows the ways in which God has revealed Himself to us and explains the attributes, plans and purposes of God. Then each attribute is related practically to the reader. This book takes you into the very heart of God and demonstrates how to draw near to Him.

RADICAL CHRISTIAN LIVING

This book explains how you can grow to become a mature Christian and help others do so as well. You'll learn the pathway to Christian maturity and how to select and train others in personal follow-up and discipling at different levels of Christian growth.

SEATED IN HEAVENLY PLACES

This book helps the reader learn how to live the victorious Christian life and walk in the power of God. It explains how to minister to others, wear the armor of God and exercise spiritual authority.

BLOW THE TRUMPET IN ZION

This book explains the dramatic story of God's covenant plan for Israel, including their past glory and suffering, their present crisis and their future hope.

JESUS IN THE FEASTS OF ISRAEL

This book is a study of the Old Testament feasts showing how they pointed to Jesus, as well as their personal and prophetic significance for today's world. The book points out how the Feasts represent seven steps to Christian growth and the peace, power and rest of God.

HOW TO PREPARE FOR THE COMING REVIVAL

There is a great expectancy in the hearts of believers everywhere that we are on the threshold of a great revival that will soon shake the world. This book explains the true meaning of revival and what we must do to prepare ourselves for a visitation from God.

SUPERNATURAL PRAYER AND FASTING

In this book Richard uses his clear writing style, God's Word and personal experiences to help us develop a supernatural prayer life.

THE HOUSE THAT GOD BUILT

by Dr. Mark Hanby.

This is a book about the Church that Jesus is building. It's not too much like the church we see in the earth today. This Church is pure, holy, loving, and full of integrity. The Church that God built will not be defeated, overcome, or discouraged. It is a Church where Jesus is Lord over all.

TPB-140p. ISBN 1-56043-091-5
Retail $7.95

PERCEIVING THE WHEEL OF GOD

by Dr. Mark Hanby.

Many have wondered about the purpose of suffering. In this book Dr. Hanby provides us with an anointed answer to that question. As unformed clay yields to the squeezing fingers of the potter, so must we perceive and yield to the wheel of God.

TPB-112p. ISBN 1-56043-109-1
Retail $7.95

To order toll free call:
Destiny Image
1-800-722-6774

BOOK ORDER FORM

Ordering Instructions

To order books, check the appropriate box, then clip and mail the coupon below to SOUNDS OF THE TRUMPET, INC., 8230 BIRCHGLENN, HOUSTON, TX 77070.

☐ Please send me ____ copy(ies) of THE MIRACLE OF THE SCARLET THREAD. I have enclosed $7.95 contribution for each copy ordered (price includes shipping).

☐ Please send me ____ copy(ies) of COME AND DINE. I have enclosed $7.95 contribution for each copy ordered (price includes shipping).

☐ Please send me ____ copy(ies) of WHAT EVERYONE NEEDS TO KNOW ABOUT GOD. I have enclosed $7.95 contribution for each copy ordered (price includes shipping).

☐ Please send me ____ copy(ies) of RADICAL CHRISTIAN LIVING. I have enclosed $7.95 contribution for each copy ordered (price includes shipping).

☐ Please send me ____ copy(ies) of SEATED IN HEAVENLY PLACES. I have enclosed $7.95 contribution for each copy ordered (price includes shipping).

☐ Please send me ____ copy(ies) of BLOW THE TRUMPET IN ZION. I have enclosed $7.95 contribution for each copy ordered (price includes shipping).

☐ Please send me ____ copy(ies) of JESUS IN THE FEASTS OF ISRAEL. I have enclosed $7.95 contribution for each copy ordered (price includes shipping).

☐ Please send me ____ copy(ies) of HOW TO PREPARE FOR THE COMING REVIVAL. I have enclosed $7.95 contribution for each copy ordered (price includes shipping).

☐ Please send me ____ copy(ies) of SUPERNATURAL PRAYER AND FASTING. I have enclosed $7.95 contribution for each copy ordered (price includes shipping).

☐ Foreign order please include an extra $2.00 per book for surface postage.

Name _____

Street _____

City _____

State _____ Zip _____

Ordering Instructions

To order tapes, check the appropriate box, then clip and mail the coupon below to SOUNDS OF THE TRUMPET, INC., 8230 BIRCHGLENN, HOUSTON, TX 77070.

. . . .

☐   Please send me the following tapes. I have enclosed a $4.00 contribution for each tape ordered (No C.O.D.), plus $2.00 for mailing for each tape series.

☐ The Bible Series   ($32.00)
☐ Getting to Know God – 1 ($16.00)
☐ Getting to Know God – 2 ($20.00)
☐ Getting to Know God – 3 ($16.00)
☐ Blood Covenant Series   ($24.00)
☐ Abundant Life Series   ($24.00)
☐ The Church Series   ($24.00)
☐ Christian Family Series   ($16.00)
☐ Faith & Healing Series   ($12.00)
☐ End Time Series   ($32.00)
☐ Get Your Prayers Answered ($24.00)
☐ Foundational Studies–1   ($24.00)

☐ Foundational Studies–2 ($24.00)
☐ The Feasts Series   ($24.00)
☐ The Sacrifices Series   ($20.00)
☐ Ephesians Series   ($48.00)
☐ Philippians Series   ($32.00)
☐ Colossians Series   ($32.00)
☐ Thessalonians Series   ($32.00)
☐ Single Messages (Circle)
    (SM 1,2,3,4,5,6,7   ($4.00 each)
    8,9,10,11,12,13
    14,15,16,17,18)
☐ Practical Studies–1   ($24.00)
☐ Practical Studies–2   ($24.00)

Name _____

Street _____

City _____

State _____ Zip _____